'We strongly recommend this book. It provides answers to important
questions on real life issues that every parent, carer or practitioner
might face today or in the future. A great read and an important addition
to sex education literature.'

– Ioannis Voskopoulos and Labrini Ioannou, Psychologists

of related interest

The Growing Up Guide for Girls
What Girls on the Autism Spectrum Need to Know!
Davida Hartman
Illustrated by Margaret Anne Suggs
ISBN 978 1 84905 574 1
eISBN 978 1 78450 038 2

The Growing Up Book for Boys
What Boys on the Autism Spectrum Need to Know!
Davida Hartman
Illustrated by Margaret Anne Suggs
ISBN 978 1 84905 575 8
eISBN 978 1 78450 039 9

Sexuality and Severe Autism
A Practical Guide for Parents, Caregivers and Health Educators
Kate E. Reynolds
ISBN 978 1 84905 327 3
eISBN 978 0 85700 666 0

Sexuality and Safety with Tom and Ellie series
Books for Young People with Autism and Related Conditions
Kate E. Reynolds
Illustrated by Jonathon Powell

What's Happening to Tom?
A book about puberty for boys and young men with autism and related conditions
ISBN 978 1 84905 523 9
eISBN 978 0 85700 934 0

Tom Needs to Go
A book about how to use public toilets safely for boys and
young men with autism and related conditions
ISBN 978 1 84905 521 5
eISBN 978 0 85700 935 7

Things Tom Likes
A book about sexuality and masturbation for boys and young
men with Autism and Related Conditions
ISBN 978 1 84905 522 2
eISBN 978 0 85700 933 3

What's Happening to Ellie?
A book about puberty for girls and young women with autism and related conditions
ISBN 978 1 84905 526 0
eISBN 978 0 85700 937 1

Ellie Needs to Go
A book about how to use public toilets safely for girls and
young women with autism and related conditions
ISBN 978 1 84905 524 6
eISBN 978 0 85700 938 8

Things Ellie Likes
A book about sexuality and masturbation for girls and young
women with autism and related conditions
ISBN 978 1 84905 525 3
eISBN 978 0 85700 936 4

WHEN YOUNG PEOPLE WITH INTELLECTUAL DISABILITIES AND AUTISM HIT PUBERTY

A PARENTS' Q&A GUIDE TO HEALTH, SEXUALITY AND RELATIONSHIPS

FREDDY JACKSON BROWN AND SARAH BROWN

Foreword by Professor Richard Hastings
Illustrations by Andy James

WITHDRAWN

Jessica Kingsley *Publishers*
London and Philadelphia

First published in 2016
by Jessica Kingsley Publishers
73 Collier Street
London N1 9BE, UK
and
400 Market Street, Suite 400
Philadelphia, PA 19106, USA

www.jkp.com

Library of Congress Cataloging in Publication Data
Names: Jackson Brown, Freddy, author.
Title: When young people with intellectual disabilities and autism hit
puberty : a parents' Q&A guide to health, sexuality and relationships /
Freddy Jackson Brown and Sarah Brown ; foreword by Professor Richard
Hastings.
Description: London ; Philadelphia : Jessica Kingsley Publishers, 2016.
Identifiers: LCCN 2015050923 | ISBN 9781849056489 (alk. paper)
Subjects: LCSH: Sex instruction for children with mental disabilities. |
Autistic youth--Sexual behavior. | Developmentally disabled youth--Sexual
behavior. | Sexual health.
Classification: LCC HQ57.2 .J33 2016 | DDC 613.9/50874--
dc23 LC record available at http://lccn.loc.gov/2015050923

British Library Cataloguing in Publication Data
A CIP catalogue record for this book is available from the British Library

ISBN 978 1 84905 648 9
eISBN 978 1 78450 216 4

Printed and bound in the United States

CONTENTS

FOREWORD

This book is written by practitioners in the field of intellectual disability and autism who have direct experience of advising families about puberty and sexuality in young people with disabilities. The book is deliberately practical, and based on questions about sexuality and puberty that parents themselves suggested. The authors' style is to tackle these questions directly and openly, and with advice about what parents (and other family carers) can do and say.

You might ask why it is important to write such a practical book for parents of young people with intellectual disability or autism. Why not a book for professionals, or even for young people themselves? The answer is grounded in findings from research I carried out with Professor Andrew Jahoda and Dr Jaycee Pownall (at the University of Glasgow) a few years ago. We noted that research on sexuality and sexual understanding in adolescents and young adults with intellectual disabilities had often focused on the knowledge of the young people themselves, and sometimes on training/teaching approaches that can help young people to increase their sexual knowledge. This work is important, but we believed that existing research neglected to understand the role of the family as the main source of information and support for young people with intellectual disabilities in particular. Jaycee and Andrew's earlier research had suggested that young people with intellectual disabilities tended to rely much more heavily on their family for information about sex than did young people with physical disabilities or no disability.

This reliance on family members makes sense of course. In the follow-on research, we found that some parents of young people with intellectual disabilities avoided talking about sex with their son or daughter, some thought that sexuality was not relevant to their son/daughter, and many lacked confidence in how to approach topics that they were embarrassed about themselves. Parents lacked practical guidance about what to do. That is where this new book comes into the picture. Given the importance of family members as a source of information about sexuality for young people with intellectual disabilities or autism, parents cannot avoid tackling the issue. At the same time, the task is not straightforward, and accurate and practical advice is needed to help parents with this task. This new book fills that gap for parents, and I commend the authors on a job well done.

Richard P. Hastings PhD CPsychol FBPsS
FIASSIDD FAcSS Professor
Cerebra Chair of Family Research
Monash Warwick Professor (Department of
Psychiatry, Monash University, Australia)

Chapter 1

THE IMPORTANCE OF SEX EDUCATION

When I (FJB) was in my mid-20s, I remember talking with a friend about how we first learned about sex. She said that as a child her parents had told her nothing about her body, puberty or sex, and she never spoke directly with her friends about these issues either. This was before she could look things up on the Internet, so, by the time she became an adolescent, she knew very little about the subject. She had learned about menstruation from listening to her friends talking amongst themselves, otherwise she knew very little before she began to have sexual contact with boys. She described how her first sexual experiences were in part exciting, bewildering and, at times, quite frightening.

Unsurprisingly she became pregnant while still a teenager and it was her first contact with her GP that brought home to her how little she knew about her body and sexual reproduction. She remembered hearing her GP explaining how she would give birth through her vaginal canal and she was dumbfounded. Up until that point she had thought her baby would be born through her belly button. She was too embarrassed to say anything at the time, but she realised that she knew almost nothing about her own body.

I recall being quite shocked by this story and I must have said something daft or insensitive because she frowned and asked me how I first found out about sex. That stumped me. I had never thought about it before that moment. And when I did, I was quite surprised as I pieced together my history, which went something like this. When I was around 10 years old, I remember some boys saying things to me about men and women 'shagging', but it didn't make sense and it scared me a little. I didn't really want to hear it and I ran away. My parents never sat me down to tell me about sex and I continued to pick up bits of information here and there. I remembered spending one summer, when I was 14 years old, talking intensely with a friend about sex as we tried to understand more about it. We thought we were piecing it all together, but the truth was between us we didn't know anything and we learned nothing new.

Around that time in school we had a 'sex education' lesson, which involved watching a short film about sexual intercourse (which we'd covered a bit in biology lessons with other animals) and human reproduction. It also showed a baby being born, which brought a silence to the room. But good as this short film was, it could only cover a small part of the subject matter. And that was the sum total of my sex education before I had my first romantic and sexual experiences. It is fair to say I wasn't well prepared.

My experiences do not appear to be unusual. A UK survey undertaken in 2007 sampling the experiences of over 20,000 young people aged under 18 found that 40 per cent said the sex and relationships education they had received at school was either poor or very poor (UK Youth Parliament 2007). And 61 per cent of boys and 70 per cent of girls said that they had been given no information about how to conduct personal relationships while at school. An expert on sex education in the UK, Professor Michael Reiss, concludes that as things presently stand we learn relatively little about sex and relationships from our schooling and instead learn it mostly from our friends (who are often as ignorant as we are) and increasingly from the media and Internet.

Does it matter how we find out about our sexuality or how to conduct ourselves in relationships? Yes and no. While some people might not have any problems with their emerging sexuality in spite of having very little formal sex and relationships education, the opposite is also true. Other people can encounter quite serious problems that could have been avoided with just a little education and information. And this is the central premise of this book – it is the idea that by providing young people with a little support, information and skills training, we can help them deal with the practical or emotional difficulties they are experiencing.

We believe good information and learning opportunities are particularly important for disabled children, many of whom face additional barriers (e.g. communication, physical, social) and will not be able to access mainstream sources. It is for those children and their families that we have written this book.

Sex education in the UK

Every single living person who has ever lived on this planet is the product of sex.[1] Sex is fundamental to life, and at certain points it plays a bit part in our lives. And yet we do not want what we do every day to be dominated by sexual behaviour. There is a time and a place for sexual activity and this is decided by the rules we make together in our society and culture. The challenge we collectively face is how we teach our children about the biology of sex and the behavioural rules we have agreed in our society.

Education is the term we generally use to describe how we teach our children (and each other) about the things that we think they need to know. And, more specifically, sex education is how we teach our children what is important about human sexuality, including our biology and interpersonal behaviour. And importantly this includes how to help them keep themselves and others safe while also enjoying all that their sexuality can mean.

---

1   Even children born via in vitro fertilisation (IVF), while not the product of human sexual intercourse, are the product of human sexual processes.

Sex and relationships education (SRE) has been a controversial, and hence political, subject for a long time in the UK. Some sex education publications were published before the 20th century, but these were mostly focused on topics such as hygiene, modesty and self-control. It was the publication of *Married Love* by Marie Stopes (Stopes 1918) that showed there was a huge interest in this area. After being turned down by multiple publishers, when it was finally published it sold out immediately, had its sixth printing within a fortnight and went on to sell more than 750,000 copies by 1931. Marie Stopes was a campaigner for equal rights for women and birth control, and unsurprisingly the book presented a new perspective on female sexuality. For instance, it was the first book to discuss openly women's sexual desires in relation to the menstrual cycle and argued for equal relationships between men and women in marriage.

Marie Stopes was ahead of her time and, in spite of being a huge success with the public, her book was criticised and ignored by the political and professional leaders of the day. While normal people were interested in the subject of sex and relationships, officialdom and the government were set on actively resisting any discussion of the topic. D.H. Lawrence's *Lady Chatterley's Lover*, for example, was famously censored when it was published in 1928 for its explicit descriptions of sex and the use of sexual words. As late as 1960 its publisher, Penguin Books, was prosecuted under the Obscene Publications Act.

In the 1950s sex education had moved on a little, though it was limited to describing the reproduction process and, as a consequence, it took place in biology lessons. And even though boys were clearly part of the equation, sex education programmes were seen as suitable mostly for girls. With the changing attitudes towards sex in the 1960s and 1970s, sex education programmes in schools slowly became more accepted and widespread. Textbooks became more detailed and included information about wider issues such as birth control, contraception and the roles of men and women in society.

By the time HIV/AIDS appeared in the 1980s, sex education programmes were commonplace in schools and followed a basic skills development model. The fact that there was no treatment for HIV/AIDS was a shock to society, as it had assumed antibiotics would control all sexually transmitted diseases. The emergence of HIV/AIDS brought a new public health dimension to sex education programmes, which raised the profile of the subject matter. While this was welcomed by campaigners, the increased focus on sex education also led to an increased level of political involvement in programme content and delivery. This has continued up to the present.

Today there is a broad consensus in the UK that sex education programmes (i.e. teaching our children about their bodies and emerging sexuality) is important. For instance, as part of the National Curriculum SRE is compulsory from age 11 onwards in our schools. This involves teaching children about puberty, reproduction, relationships, sexuality and sexual health, and it plays an important part in increasing their understanding of these matters.

While National Curriculum guidance is welcome, its current SRE content and timing has been criticised by leading campaign groups, like the Sex Education Forum[2] as offering our children too little information, too late. For instance, schools are advised to teach Key Stage 3 children (i.e. 11–14 years old) about the menstrual cycle but without information about sexual health, hormones and sexually transmitted disease. Contraception is not included for Key Stage 3 children and there is no requirement to teach primary school children the proper names for external genitalia.

While history tells us that human sexuality, and sex education in particular, have always been political issues (after all politics is the process by which we decide how to live together), campaigners have been critical of what they see as the over-politicisation of SRE programmes in the UK. Compared with other countries, such as Sweden or the

---

2   www.sexeducationforum.org.uk.

Netherlands, where sex education is focused more on teaching children and young people about their bodies and healthy interpersonal behaviour, the UK has up to ten times higher rates of teenage pregnancy.

We believe that no child should experience her first period or his first wet dream without knowing about it ahead of time. It's just too scary. Start talking with your child about puberty before it begins, and then continue the discussions all throughout puberty.

Child development, sexuality and disability

Child development is a complex process and it is all the more complex when a child has a disability. All the 'normal' developmental milestones and achievements become less certain as the child takes a more unique path through life. Parents have told us that this is one of the hardest things about raising a child with a disability.

The uncertainty surrounding if or when a disabled child will learn a particular skill can undermine confidence in knowing what to do when a child is struggling to do something. Is this because she can't do it, or just doesn't want to do it? We know more or less when a typically developing child can or should be able to control her bladder or brush her teeth, but what about with a disabled child? For instance, when a 5-year-old with good continence skills wets herself on the sofa while watching a favourite TV programme, we do not hesitate to tell her off. We know she has the skill – she has just chosen not to use it at that point in time. But what happens with a 4-year-old physically or intellectually disabled child? Does she have the ability to fully control her bladder? Does she really understand what is happening? Can she get to the toilet independently? At that moment all these questions, and many more, might go through a parent's mind.

An important developmental area for disabled children (like all children) is sexuality. Unless they have a particular genetic or medical condition, as they grow older they will enter puberty at some stage. For some disabled children this can be very early (e.g. 5 years), for others it can be very late (e.g. 20 years), but either way, it will come. And when it comes, a new dimension will be added to their character as a new motivation enters their life – the motivation for sexual and romantic relationships with other people.

Just like everybody else, what sex and sexuality mean for a disabled child or young person will vary. For some people sex is a minor issue, almost irrelevant, and for others it is almost all they think about. How interested or motivated people are with regard to sex varies in unpredictable ways. The only thing we know for sure is that there is a wide spectrum of human responses to sex. In the opening chapter of his book *How Sexual Desire Works* (2014), Professor Frederick Toates asks if there is a healthy norm for sexual appetites? And if so, do deviations from this norm indicate some kind of problem or disorder? Unsurprisingly there is no single answer to this because what represents the 'norm' is also affected by social influences and culture. Genghis Khan, for instance, reputedly fathered hundreds of offspring, such that geneticists today have identified as many as 16 million people carrying his Y chromosome. By modern standards this behaviour would be seen as deviant, but at the time it was respected as the behaviour of an honoured emperor.

How we judge behaviour, sexual or otherwise, depends on when and where it occurs. This is particularly important for disabled children, who may express their sexuality inappropriately in public places or with inappropriate people. A child might masturbate in class at school, make lewd comments in the street or send naked pictures of themselves to their teacher or friends. These behaviours are problematic because they break many of society's rules about how we display our sexuality and behave towards each other. And ultimately social rules about how we should behave in public are codified in our civil and criminal laws, with accompanying sanctions for breaking them.

Why is it difficult to talk about sex?

A parent's job can be split into three main areas – to keep their children safe, to feed and nourish them and to help them learn about the world and the skills they need to be successful in it. This book is most interested in the first and third elements – how to help children and young people keep safe in today's society and, simultaneously, how to learn to express and deal with their own sexuality in a healthy way.

As a child grows, we teach them a range of skills, like how to communicate, how to feed themselves, how to use the toilet, how to get dressed, how to play and tidy up afterwards, how to catch balls, how to be polite and a lot more besides. In short we teach them about all the things they need to know in order to be as independent as possible. How much a disabled child can learn will vary of course, with some children being able to use the toilet by the age of 3 and others needing help for the rest of their lives, for instance. But irrespective of what a child is able to do for themselves or how much support they need, the basic tasks of parenthood remain the same – keep them safe, feed them and help them learn as much as they can. And this includes learning about reproduction, sexuality and sexual health.

While everyone would accept that learning about sexuality and relationships is important, it is also the case that teaching our children about this subject is difficult. Why is this? Part of the reason is privacy. For most people sex is an intensely personal and private matter that we share only with those we love. Although this is not a problem in itself, this fact does make it difficult for us to talk about it openly. It is quite natural to feel awkward and embarrassed when the topic of sex comes up in public as it's not a public topic, except perhaps in the form of jokes and humour. Another part of the reason is that a parent's relationship with their child is not a sexual one. For psychological, social and genetic reasons, a parent should never be a child's sexual partner. This is something our society takes very seriously and it is a good thing we do because incest is both psychologically and genetically damaging.

But one unavoidable consequence of increasing the taboo about parent–child sexual contact is to make it harder for parents to talk with their children about sex. These two factors probably go a long way to explaining why it is so difficult to talk with our children about sex.

Human beings, like all living things, will try to avoid or minimise unpleasant or negative events. Avoidance is a very useful response because basically we have a better chance of survival if we move away from things that make us feel bad. So it is no surprise then that we will want to avoid discussing sexuality with our children because of the unpleasant emotions of embarrassment and awkwardness it raises in us. Feeling embarrassed and awkward is unpleasant and, when possible, we do our best to avoid it because that is how we typically respond to negative things.

The problem is that avoidance can stop us doing important things. Avoidance might alleviate our feelings of embarrassment in the short term, but it doesn't solve the problem in the medium or longer term. Our child still needs to learn about their sexuality and how to develop positive relationships and if we don't help them with this, then who will?

I recall seeing a provocative poster at my GP surgery, which asked: 'Where do you want your child to learn about sex? 1. Their friends? 2. Pornography? 3. You?' Of course, there are other options, but the basic point was made. If we do not teach our children about their sexuality and how to conduct themselves in relationships, then they will learn these lessons elsewhere in uncontrolled, potentially problematic ways. This position can be summed up with the old maxim, 'If you think education is expensive, then try ignorance'.

Chapter 2

WHY READ THIS BOOK?

HEALTHY DEVELOPMENT AND KEEPING SAFE

There are many reasons to read this book. You might be concerned about some aspect of your child's sexual development or behaviour, or just want to know more about how to support them in this area. Whatever your motivation, it is likely to raise some difficult and thought provoking issues for you. For most people sexual behaviour is an intensely personal and private experience and this means we find it hard to speak about in public. It can be particularly challenging for a parent to think about their disabled child's sexual development. As a consequence this important area often isn't talked about openly. This book is an attempt to rectify this.

We want to provide some ideas about what might be happening as your child grows up with disabilities and what you can do to support them, so that you can decide how you want to approach issues around growing up, sex and relationships. We have focused on common concerns around sexuality and growing up that parents have discussed with us in our clinical practice, some of which may seem familiar and some more unusual.

It is quite natural to feel uncomfortable in relation to your child's sexuality, and that is okay. You can still make a choice to support your child even when you are feeling uncomfortable. This is important because you will be your child's main carer as they move into adulthood. No matter how good schools and other professionals are, issues to do with growing up, sexual development and relationships are just too important to be left to them alone. For a start, parents know their children best and can provide the continuity of message across the years that young people need. It is parents and carers who are the cornerstone of their child's learning and healthy development.

This book describes how we can support young people with disabilities to learn the skills they need to maximise their independence and express their sexuality in healthy and positive ways.

Sexual abuse and 'thinking the unthinkable'

One particularly important issue for disabled people is sexual abuse. While reliable data are hard to come by, all the research indicates that disabled people are more vulnerable to being sexually abused. And a parallel fact (though uncomfortable) is that disabled people are also most likely to be the perpetrators of sexual assaults on other disabled people. We believe part of the reason for this is disabled young people with intellectual disabilities have often missed out on critical skills training and support with their sexual behaviour.

The possibility of sexual abuse of children with disabilities is a major fear for parents/carers of children, particularly when they need support with intimate care or handling. This can be such an uncomfortable thought that people can shy away from having it. This is a mistake. In the 1980s Ann Craft and Hilary Brown coined the phrase 'thinking the unthinkable' to encourage people to consider the possibility of abuse (Brown and Craft 1989). To protect people with disabilities from sexual abuse, we need first to acknowledge that it can and does happen, and sadly the perpetrators can be those in a trusted role.

Kitson highlights that people (and children) with intellectual disabilities can be more 'vulnerable' for some of the reasons set out below:

- poor verbal and non-verbal communication

- lack of knowledge and information

- dependence on support with personal intimate care

- being cared for by a number of different carers in different environments

- not being believed or listened to

- having a limited understanding of risk

- being unaware of their right to say 'no' or complain.

This book will address some of these vulnerabilities and provide some guidance for what can be done to increase your children's safety and safe behaviour.

Principles for keeping safe

While we can never reduce risks in life to zero, there are things we can do to help keep disabled children safe. This doesn't mean we can completely stop bad things happening, but it does mean we can make them less likely. Below are some of the key principles that we will look at throughout this book:

- Improving communication skills: The more children can communicate, the more they can tell us about their lives. When they learn to label their emotions, they can tell us when they are feeling happy or sad. By empowering them to make choices, they can have more confidence to make and break relationships. By teaching children to label their body parts accurately, they can tell us where they have been touched.

- Teaching essential living skills: By teaching them to distinguish 'public' and 'private', they will start to know the social rules in our society in relation to sexual behaviour. If we teach children how to wash themselves as independently as possible, they will be less reliant on other adults in their life and have a sense of control over their bodies.

- Being emotionally supportive: How we respond to children's needs as they enter puberty will affect how they understand their emerging sexuality. If we respond to early signs of sexual behaviour with understanding (even when we are uncomfortable) rather than disapproval or discomfort, we will let them know that that they can enjoy their bodies and feelings safely. If we respond to young people's emerging sexual interest in other young people with openness and support, they will be able to express their sexuality and not repress it, and know that they are likeable and loveable.

- Understanding personal care needs: Thinking about how personal care happens, who provides it and how we acknowledge children's preferences is important. If we consider providing a running commentary as we are providing personal care, we give a message that what's happening to their body is important, and that they can communicate 'stop' if they want to. If we give young people an opportunity to choose who provides personal care as they grow up, we show them that they can have some control over their body and their privacy.

- Supporting positive relationships: Thinking about where young children and young people can meet each other allows them to develop connections, friendships and relationships as independently as possible. We can decide how and when young people will have opportunities to be alone with their peers and have access to privacy as they grow up.

- Listening to what children and young people say: This might sound obvious, but it can be harder than you think! Really listening to children and taking seriously what they say enables them to take more control over their lives. When we listen to children, we encourage them to take charge of their lives. They learn to make their own independent decisions; children can also begin to have the confidence to communicate 'no' to unwanted sexual contact, to accept touch and communicate 'no' to touch that is unwanted.

SAFEGUARDING NOTE: Sometimes sexualised behaviour can be a sign that children have had sexualised experiences and they are doing to others that which has been done to them. These may or may not be abusive experiences. It is important not to panic but to consider whether this behaviour is happening alongside other changes, such as changes in mood, behaviour or physical health.

To talk or not to talk...

The above principles all require that we communicate with children and young people. You might be thinking that this is all very well, but my child has a severe intellectual disability – are you sure it is appropriate to talk to her about her body, sexuality and relationships?

In our experience a common dilemma for parents is whether it is better to talk or not to talk to their children about their developing bodies, sexuality and relationships. What if it confuses them or sets up unrealistic expectations? What is the point if in all likelihood they may never have a chance for a private sexual life or relationship because of the physical/social/emotional challenges related to their disability? It is quite natural to worry that talking about something valued in society that they might not have access to (like romantic relationships) will make them feel 'different' and cause them pain. Indeed we've even heard professionals say 'if they don't ask, then don't tell'.

We hold a different view. Our approach is based on an idea that sexuality and relationships are relevant to *all* young people. If we think of sexuality as a spectrum, from social connections and expressing feelings at the one end, to developing intimate and sexual relationships at the other, we see that we all have a place on the spectrum somewhere. Deciding what it is that children need to know is up to you as a family as each child will have different needs. As a rule, we think that children need access to as much information, skills training and support as they can assimilate, when they are ready for it. They may need this information broken down, and repeated opportunities to learn communication and daily living skills. That can make the process harder, but it is no less important.

If we support children and young people to understand their bodies, to form healthy relationships and to express their sexuality positively, we can help them enjoy this part of their lives as much as possible. This doesn't mean there will be no difficulties or pain along the way. There will be, just like there are for everyone else. But it does mean we can keep these events to a minimum and help them to live their lives as fully, safely and healthily as possible.

Chapter 3

BIOLOGY, BODIES AND GROWING UP WITH INTELLECTUAL DISABILITIES

Adolescence and puberty can be a difficult time for children whether they have an intellectual disability or not. They might not understand or like the changes that are happening in their bodies and this can be the source of embarrassment and fear. While puberty can't be avoided, we believe that it's just not necessary for a child to experience their first period or their first wet dream without knowing what is happening to them. With support, education and learning opportunities, the difficulties that puberty brings can be kept to a minimum and children can grow and develop healthily.

This chapter will describe in broad terms what happens biologically to our bodies as we enter puberty and the particular issues facing young people with intellectual disabilities as they grow into adults. It will provide basic information about what is happening in your child's body as they enter puberty, and looks at some of the additional challenges they may face as they move through this phase of life.

The biology of puberty

Puberty refers to the period of human development when our bodies reach sexual maturity and we become capable of reproduction. It is not known what triggers the start of puberty, but once started it is a period of great change. During puberty the hypothalamus stimulates the pituitary gland to release hormones called gonadotropins into the bloodstream.

These hormones (basically chemical messages) lead to the production of oestrogen and androgen in both boys and girls (though girls have higher levels of oestrogen and boys have higher levels of androgen), which change the body.

Puberty doesn't begin at a fixed age, but it usually takes place between the ages of 8 and 13 years and lasts for 2 to 5 years. This can vary for children with intellectual disabilities, who can start earlier and later than this. If you child starts puberty before the age of 8 years, it is a good idea to discuss this with your GP.

The hormones that are released in puberty lead to a number of bodily changes, such as growth, pubic hair, acne, menstruation and genital maturation.

Changes in females

- Bodily growth: Bodies grow taller and heavier during puberty (sometimes called a 'growth spurt'). Bones thicken, muscles develop and fat increases around the hips (which widen to produce a wider birth canal), breasts, arms and legs (see Figure 3.1).

- Breast development: This is usually the first physical sign of puberty and usually begins between 8 and 13 years of age. Breast size naturally varies from woman to woman.

- Pubic and body hair: Hair grows and thickens around the vagina to form an inverted triangle and this often continues for years after it first starts. Hair also begins to grow under the arms.

- Menstruation (often called 'periods'): Menstruation is the discharge of blood and the lining of the uterus through the vagina. It usually occurs on a monthly cycle. Most girls have their first period around 11–13 years, though it can be younger than this.

- Body odour and acne: Changing hormones alter the composition of sweat so that it is more abundant and its odour becomes stronger. These hormonal changes also affect skin condition, which can lead to acne.

Figure 3.1 Changes in the female body during puberty.

Changes in males

- Bodily growth: Bodies grow taller and heavier during puberty (sometimes called a 'growth spurt'). Bones become heavier and muscles stronger as the body begins to look more adult (Figure 3.2).

- Pubic and body hair: Hair grows around the penis and gradually becomes darker and coarser. Body hair becomes thicker and grows under the arms, and boys start to grow facial hair.

- Penis and testicular growth: Testicular growth is one of the first signs of puberty in boys as the scrotum grows larger. Pubic hair at the base of the penis accompanies this growth, and later the length and breadth of the penis increases.

- Erection: The growth of the penis means that erections (which are more common and spontaneous) become more obvious and this can be a cause of embarrassment.

- Voice change: Changes to the voice box and larynx mean that the voice will drop and deepen, often over several months. During this time the pitch of a young person's voice can vary between high and low and even sound squeaky, but don't worry as it's all part of the change process and eventually settles down.

- Body odour and acne: Changing hormones alter the composition of sweat so that it is more abundant and its odour becomes stronger. These hormonal changes also affect skin condition, and acne occurs when the hair follicles become clogged.

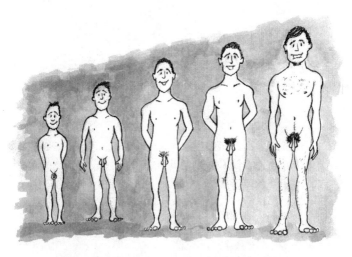

Figure 3.2 Changes in the male body during puberty.

Puberty for children with intellectual disabilities

The biological processes and bodily changes outlined above will be broadly the same for everyone. These can be hard enough on their own, but children with intellectual disabilities face additional challenges that stem from their increased difficulties in understanding what is happening and how they are feeling. To help them through this period of their life they are likely to need extra support and patience as they learn the skills they need to express their emerging sexuality and make healthy choices.

Adolescence is a difficult time for all children. They often report high levels of emotional distress as they cope with their changing bodies and expectations. Worrying about romantic relationships and their sexuality is also common. For children with intellectual disabilities, the challenges will be all the greater. The nature of their intellectual difficulties means they will struggle to understand what is happening to their bodies and to communicate their needs. This can, in turn, lead to a range of inappropriate behaviours that leave them at risk of criticism, rejection or even abuse. For example, they may not fully understand the importance of privacy and so masturbate in public whenever the urge arises. Or they may want to have a romantic relationship with someone and instead of asking them on a date, they tease or grope them. Learning socially acceptable ways to express their sexuality and communicate what they want is a critical skill, which they may struggle to learn. Or they may never be able to learn these skills and require permanent support with this aspect of who they are.

Puberty can also be a challenging time for parents. Watching your child's body change into its adult form can be an emotional time, filled with both positive and negative emotions. Finding the right time and words to talk about the changes that accompany puberty can be difficult and sometimes embarrassing. How will they cope with menstruation, erections, masturbation, sexual desire, and what about the highs and lows of romantic relationships? Will they find a suitable partner and, if not, how will they cope with the pain of rejection? These issues will throw up all sorts of challenging questions, like should your child be taught to masturbate to orgasm and, if so, how? Or how do you support your child to have a private romantic relationship that might involve sexual behaviour?

At the same time, your child may start to be more oppositional as they try to assert their own independence as an 'emerging adult'. The period of adolescence is famous for its discord between the generations, and children with intellectual disabilities will behave in similar ways. Almost inevitably the child's desire to grow and be independent will clash with the parents' instinct to protect their children.

Supporting your child through adolescence and puberty is no easy task and it might be tempting to minimise the issue and ignore your child's emerging sexuality. The simplest way to keep them safe and healthy after all is to restrict their opportunities to meet other young people. Or you might hope that if you don't teach them about their sexuality, then they won't show any interest in this area. But in our experience this strategy rarely works and instead can lead to other problems further down the line. Difficult as it is, we have to find a way to support positive sexual behaviours and risk taking as they explore this part of themselves.

As your child embarks on their journey into puberty and beyond, it is important to recognise that it will take years and there will be many up and downs along the way. When difficulties arise (and they will), do not worry if they can't be solved immediately. Solutions will often involve learning new self-management and communication skills, and this will take time. So when issues arise, take your time to understand what is happening before planning carefully how to respond.

We hope that this book will answer some of the questions you might have during your child's journey through adolescence. But of course the best way to deal with problems is to prevent them occurring in the first place. And this means providing our children with educational learning programmes that teach them about what is happening to them and how they can express their sexuality in positive and socially appropriate ways.

Chapter 4

BODIES

This chapter presents questions that families often ask about how to support their children as their bodies change during puberty. It looks at different issues and problems that can arise as children grow into their adult bodies.

4.1 I'm worried about my child starting puberty. What can I do to help?

Puberty is the series of physical changes that every child goes through as they develop towards adulthood and their body gets ready to be able to make a baby. Puberty usually happens between the ages of 10 and 16. For girls, periods usually start between the ages of 11 and 14, though this varies and some girls will start sooner and some later. For children with conditions such as cerebral palsy, there can be even wider variation in the age that puberty starts, as well as how long it takes to complete. Sometimes children with cerebral palsy start puberty sooner, but take longer to complete their development. There are some genetic conditions that are associated with differences in how puberty happens; for example, young people with Prader–Willi syndrome may have differences in their sex organs and the start of puberty may be delayed.

DEFINITIONS

Puberty starts when hormones are released that kick off a series of changes in a child's body. The first signs of puberty for girls are usually changes to their breasts, the start of body odour and hair growing under their arms and between their legs. Next they might notice some vaginal discharge. Periods are the sign that a girl's body is getting ready to be able to have a baby. They happen every month when an egg travels down the fallopian tubes to the womb. If the egg is not fertilised, then the lining of the womb breaks down and leaves the body as blood through the vagina. Premenstrual tension (sometimes called premenstrual syndrome) can happen a few says before a girl's period. It can lead to symptoms including mood swings, cramping in the stomach area, headaches, and tiredness. See Chapter 3 for more information about puberty.

> Dawn is 8 years old and her mother has started to notice some early signs of puberty, including body odour and small breast buds (lumps) behind her nipples. She is concerned that her daughter is very young – emotionally she sees her as a 5- or 6-year-old rather than an 8-year-old.

What's the issue?

In Western culture, puberty can be seen as something to celebrate, just like other developmental milestones (such as walking and talking), as it is a positive sign that a young person is growing up. Being grown up is usually associated with exciting things, like going out with friends, buying bras, having boyfriends or girlfriends and falling in love. Young people often feel proud of the changes to their body and can be anxious for things to change so that they can be 'like everyone else'. At the same time, puberty starting early can be a concern for parents who feel that their child isn't emotionally or socially ready in their development to understand and manage the changes to their body. It can be hard for parents who worry about managing their child's behaviour and how they will react to things like seeing blood come out of their vagina or wet dreams.

What can we do?

1 Help your child to understand what's normal and what to expect

All children feel confused to some degree when their bodies are changing during puberty. Even though it can be more difficult to explain to children with intellectual disabilities what is happening, they still need to know as much as possible. Otherwise, like other children, they will come to their own (usually incorrect) conclusions about what is happening and they can feel very alone. For example, if they don't know that puberty is quite natural, children can think that something is wrong with them or that they are ill when their bodies first start to change in puberty. To help your child understand what is happening it is likely they will need information to be simplified and to be repeated in order to fully prepare them for puberty.

One way you can do this is to read stories that you think your child will understand. Dawn's parents could read her Victoria Parker's (2007) *The Little Book of Growing Up*. Or Kate Reynolds' (2015) *What's Happening to Ellie? A Book about Puberty for Girls and Young Women with Autism and Related Conditions*.

These picture books help children to understand what is happening to their bodies as they grow up in easily accessible formats. In addition to books, you can use photographs and stories about your child and the changes that have already happened to him or her, and/or other members of the family.

Talk to your child about what they looked like as a baby, what they look like now and what will change.

You can also use objects to reinforce the messages you are giving about what happens as they grow up. When you (or others) are doing the laundry, for example, ask your child to help and see if they can identify which clothes are for the boys in the house, which are for the girls and which are for the grown ups or the children. You can also start to introduce concepts such as *public* and *private* this way, by asking your child which clothes cover your private parts. Begin to show your child the things that they will need to help them keep their body clean and comfortable – for example, bras, deodorant, face wash.

Dawn's mum might need to start building in new routines for her daughter such as showering daily.

2 Teach your child the skills they require

Extra self-care skills that your son or daughter may need to acquire include:

- washing their body, including genitals and face
- managing spots
- using deodorant
- preparing for and managing periods
- shaving.

Start with helping your child to understand the products and objects associated with each of these skills, and give them a chance to choose products that they think smell nice, look nice or feel nice. For example, help your child to choose deodorant that they are likely to be able to use easily (possibly roll on rather than spray) and show them a selection of different products to choose from.

A good technique for teaching new skills is called 'backwards chaining'. This means asking your child to complete the last stage of the task only, and then the last two stages and then three stages, etc. For example, if you are teaching your daughter to shave her underarm hair, you might apply the soap for her, shave for her, then ask her to rinse off. The next time, you might apply the soap, shave one underarm for her, ask her to do the last bit of shaving for the second underarm and then ask her to rinse off. Each time, you gradually ask her to do a little bit more until you are confident that she can manage safely.

Some children might not be able to manage all of these tasks yet, but it is still a good idea to develop a teaching programme for them that supports them to be as independent as possible. If you feel that your child is still dependent on your support to manage their daily hygiene tasks, providing a running commentary and helping them to understand what you are doing to them can still be the first stages of the teaching programme.

Remember to reward your daughter's attempts at learning these skills, with things that are meaningful to her. This might be praise – a 'well done!' and high five for some children – and for others it might be extra minutes on their favourite activity.

If your child also receives support from other people with their hygiene needs, then documenting what you do together in an intimate and personal care plan can keep their support consistent. This is particularly important if they are anxious or worried about what is happening. It will also ensure that the focus of their support remains on skills development.

3 Think about communication

Communication is vitally important when supporting children with their personal hygiene or when they are learning new skills. If your child already uses visual schedules, start to include specific symbols to represent the new steps in the routine that need to happen because they are growing up. For example, in their schedule for getting dressed, include a picture or photograph of the deodorant they have chosen to use, Or if your daughter is using a schedule at school, choose an image to represent 'changing sanitary pad' for each break time, if she has her period. Some families we have worked with use a purple flower (and purple wash bag) to represent periods, but this might be too abstract for some children and they may need a photograph of a sanitary pad. Creating visual stories with pictures of what will happen can help children understand what is happening and why. Examples of social stories can be found in: Carol Gray's (2015) *The New Social Story Book*.

4.2 How do I help my child to keep clean and wash properly?

Washing to keep ourselves clean and healthy is important. Being clean, for instance, reduces our chances of suffering from stomach bugs, having skin problems or bad body odour, or worse, all three! Washing and keeping clean also matter socially. As human beings we can't help but judge people by their appearance; and when someone is dirty and hasn't washed, in today's society we tend to judge them negatively, which will inevitably impact on their social relationships and opportunities.

Strange as this may sound, it wasn't always like this. Queen Elizabeth I, for instance, was said to have one bath a year – in her words 'whether I need it or not'! By today's standards she would definitely need a long hot scrub, but for people living in the 17th century it wasn't important to bathe regularly. They didn't understand the health benefits of keeping clean and it was quite normal to smell a bit. After all, if everyone had bad body odour, then yours wouldn't stand out much!

Things are different now, but the fact is that washing daily (which is pretty normal in developed countries) is a very modern desire and dependent on our cultural context. This means it is not just something we do, like breathing; we need reasons or we just won't bother. One of the reasons I like to keep clean is so that other people will judge me positively, but what if I don't really care or notice what other people think? I also wash to stay healthy and minimise the risk of illness, but what if I don't value or understand the link between good hygiene and good health? Without these motivations, then I'm not very likely to bother to wash.

It is quite common for children with intellectual disabilities not to understand fully the importance of washing properly and keeping clean. What's more, it can be a bit of a chore and they may not like the physical sensations of water or soap, so they may have lots of reasons not to wash. When this happens, the only option is to provide extra reasons to motivate them!

Tom is 10 years old. He is growing up quickly and his mum has noticed that he is starting to go through puberty. He has started to sweat and she has noticed some body odour. Tom has a diagnosis of autism and finds it difficult to wash and look after his body himself. He doesn't really see the point in it, he hates the sensation of having his face washed and he doesn't really like the smell of the products. If left alone in the bathroom, his mum says he sits in the bath for hours without doing anything. She knows that it is important that he starts to take responsibility for washing himself but he seems to need her support as much now as he did when he was a young child.

What's the issue?

All children need support when they are learning to wash and clean their own bodies. For most children, learning happens first through play, followed then through parents/carers giving them small tasks that they are responsible for. For example, we might say: 'I'll put the soap on your hand then you wash your arms and chest.' Eventually, children learn the skills they need to wash themselves and remember the sequence of tasks. They might occasionally need a reminder from us – for example, 'Remember to wash your face properly!' But hopefully they will be motivated to please us and to receive a 'well done!'

As well as the practical challenge of washing regularly, supporting your disabled child to wash can also be emotionally difficult. We'll look at this issue in more detail in the next section.

What can we do?

Here are four main strategies for supporting young people to learn to wash and clean their bodies:

1 Explain why washing your body is important and the social consequences of doing it daily

Young people might benefit from the following messages:

- It keeps you smelling nice.

- It keeps your body healthy and keeps you feeling well.

- Other people will be happy to be close to you.

- Your body is private and not for other people to touch. If you learn to wash your body, then other people will not need to touch you.

Using pictures or simple stories can be a helpful way of explaining the social context around washing and cleaning bodies.

2 Develop additional ways of communicating expectations to children

Children may need help to remember the tasks of washing and cleaning their bodies and the sequence of these tasks. Even if children understand language and verbal prompts, they may benefit from a visual checklist or sequence of symbols in order to reduce their reliance on your running commentary.

1. Get your shower gel and flannel.

2. Fill the bath with warm water.

3. Wash your face and neck.

4. Rinse off the soap.

3 Set up the environment to support children to be independent

Prepare a set of drawers or wash bags with a set of products and items that your child needs in the right order.

Involve your child in finding products that they can tolerate such as fragrance free soaps. If your child doesn't like the feel of the shower, try using a jug for your child to pour water over their body instead of using a shower head. 'Disco showers' are shower heads with LED lights that make the water appear a certain colour to represent 'hot', 'cold' or 'just right'. They can be helpful for children who find it difficult to get the temperature of the water right or who may be hyposensitive to temperature and risk letting the water get too hot.

If it is not safe to leave your child unattended in the bathroom, consider using a privacy screen so that you can stay in the bathroom but allow your child a few minutes to wash themselves.

4 Find rewards that are motivating for your child

When your child isn't motivated by your encouragement and praise, then they will need a bit of extra motivation. This might sound straightforward, but what we find rewarding varies and changes over time.

Rewards are things that your child might want and the easiest way to find out what this might be is to ask them. If your child can talk or communicate with signs or symbols, then spend a bit of time finding out what they would like. So they don't say something too unrealistic or expensive (e.g. 'I want a new bike'), it is a good idea to identify the sorts of things they would want beforehand and maybe put them on a 'choices board'. Your child might say they want to watch television, read a book, play on the computer, play Connect4 with you, do the vacuuming (yes, that is a real reward a child once asked for!) or feed the dog (another real one). Basically anything they like doing. Before you remind them to have a wash, you can ask what they would like as their reward. Then once they complete their wash, give their rewards immediately.

If a choices board is too complicated, then give them a choice of two simple things. You might say something like: 'After you've had a bath and brushed your teeth you can have, (1) Ten minutes on the computer, or (2) Ten minutes playing with your cars/dinosaurs/dolls.'

PROBLEMS THAT CAN OCCUR

1. If your child doesn't start the process of washing, just check they know what to do. Sometimes we don't start things because we are unsure of what we should be doing. If this is the case, then go through the tasks involved again, using pictures if that helps.

2. If they know what to do but don't start, then it may be that the reward isn't motivating enough. As what we find rewarding changes over time anyway, it is likely that you will face this problem at some point. When it happens, review the rewards and check your child does actually want them. It might be time to get some new rewards on the choices board.

3. If they start the washing task but stop before they finish, then it may be that the task is too big. For instance, you might have asked them to have a bath, brush their teeth and get dressed, but they keep stopping halfway through. In this case try using a reward for each stage. This will slow things down, but at least they will be independently getting ready. And then once they've been doing this for a while, you can try reducing the rewards so your child might get a reward after doing the first two stages and then another after doing the last stage. Then a little while later you can reduce the rewards again and have a single reward at the end of the three stages.

USING REWARDS TO MOTIVATE YOUR CHILD

One important thing to remember about rewards is that big does not equal best. The most important things is that they are consistent and meaningful, not their size.

If your child can't tell you what they want by talking to you, or with signs/symbols, the best way to know what they want is to use their play preferences as a guide. Usually people spend their free time doing things they like. If your child likes watching television, playing with bubbles or doing puzzles, then those things are likely to be rewards for them in other situations. In the end the only way to really find out if they like something and will work for it as a reward is to try it out. When you do this, it is worth sticking with it for a week or so before deciding whether it works or not, as the first few times you try it the child might not understand what is going on. But overall the reward principle is the same whether your child can communicate directly what they want with you or not. The key is to find things they like and would be prepared to do a little work for.

Will I have to reward my child for washing forever? It may be the case that you will have to reward your child for each and every step of a washing programme. If that is the case, then it won't be easy and that may be what has to happen. However, in our experience, as children – even those with severe disabilities – engage in washing and self-care activities over extended periods of time, these behaviours become the routine. And more than this, these behaviours become what they expect and want to happen because they can come to enjoy the process and feeling of being clean and this just becomes normal for them.

4.3 My child has a grown up body. Should I still be helping with intimate care?

Providing personal and intimate care to babies and young children is something that is expected and absolutely necessary. We don't think twice about bathing children, changing nappies, brushing their teeth, etc. and we expect to continue this until they have developed their self-care skills. When children require this support for much longer, due to physical or intellectual disabilities, sometimes parents/carers feel the same way – that they will continue to support their children until they have the skills (whenever that may be), and sometimes parents make a decision to allow carers to provide support.

Whatever a family decides, it is completely normal for parents and carers to experience more uncomfortable feelings about providing personal care to their children with grown up bodies. For many parents, it takes time to adapt to their children developing pubic hair, starting menstruation or having wet dreams. Often, parents/carers may have only experienced needing this support themselves during periods of illness, or with elderly members of the family. This means they have to find their own way to manage this within their relationships with their children.

DEFINITIONS

Intimate care includes tasks such as washing/showering, changing continence pads, changing sanitary pads (i.e helping with intimate parts of the body). Personal care includes tasks like tooth brushing, brushing hair, prompting for the toilet (i.e helping with non-intimate parts of the body).

What's the issue?

There are lots of issues that need to be considered:

- How does your child feel about intimate care and what would they like? They may not always express this verbally, but instead show how they feel with their behaviour. For instance, they might try to be as independent as possible with their washing, indicating they do not want you to help.

- How do you feel about providing intimate care and how do you respond to these emotions?

- What skills does your child need to learn and how can you teach them?

- How do you decide when to ask others to help with personal care and how do you decide who helps your child?

- How do you ensure that your child is safe, respected and that care is provided in a consistent way?

Sam is 13. He has an intellectual disability and has some difficulties with mobility. He is able to use a urine bottle and so can urinate independently but needs some help to transfer to a toilet to defecate. At school he avoids using the toilet at all. When he's at home, he usually prefers his family to help him, and becomes irritated when they are not there to help. His mum has started to notice that he is becoming embarrassed about other people helping him with personal care. She wonders whether she could just continue to help him as this seems to be what he wants, or whether there is another way of supporting Sam.

 What can we do?

1 Develop a person-centred intimate care plan

An intimate care plan supports parents, schools and young people to make choices about who provides personal and intimate care and how. The focus is on using the plan to develop skills in intimate and personal care by documenting what the young person can already do and what they need help to work on. It clarifies what communication systems need to be in place – for example, to request help, to understand the steps in personal care or to say 'yes' or 'no' to what's happening. It also includes who will be involved in care. The plan documents any risks, such as the risk of sexual arousal happening during intimate care, and everyone's response (what they will say and do if this occurs). The plan ensures a safe and dignified approach to care.

Sam seems to be at a stage when his sense of social embarrassment is having an impact on his self-care since he is avoiding using the toilet at school. The care plan could be used with Sam to talk about who he would prefer to help him and how this can be done in a dignified way. The people supporting Sam to develop the plan could acknowledge that it is normal to go through a stage of feeling self-conscious about your body and about needing help with personal care. They could help Sam to feel that he does not have to manage these feelings alone. The plan could be helpful in documenting what Sam can currently do for himself and what equipment is required for independence in all settings.

2 Letting go vs holding on

Being faced with a grown up body often brings a dilemma for parents: how do I let them grow up whilst still protecting them? Of course, balancing 'letting go' (letting children grow up and separate from you) and 'holding on' (providing support) is a universal issue for all parents and children. For parents of children with disabilities there can sometimes be some extra obstacles to separating. Parents can find it challenging to reconcile the difference between a child having a grown up body and being emotionally and intellectually 'younger' in development. Historically in our society, people have tended to manage this by continuing to treat people with intellectual disabilities as children, and being protective.

Sam's parents could consider these questions: How will I know when or if he is ready for someone else to provide personal care? Do I want to continue providing personal care for Sam? Am I letting him grow up?

Some young people with profound and multiple intellectual disabilities will always depend on a level of care. The idea of planned dependence might be helpful in giving yourself, as a parent or carer, permission not to keep pushing and teaching the development of skills, if this is unrealistic, but to accept your child, and their needs, as they are (Carnaby 2006). Of course, if it is likely that your child will always be dependent on care, it might be that deciding to step back as a parent and allowing others to care for them might need to be planned and initiated by you, rather than waiting for your child to initiate this.

3 Involve your child in discussion about personal and intimate care

In our experience, young people are more than happy to have the opportunity to talk about how they want care to happen. If they struggle with verbal communication, then use the best communication method for them – for example, using visual symbols or drawings.

Discussions may happen around:

- Who would they like and not like to help them with personal and intimate care?

- How will they ask for help and what will happen?

- What equipment and materials will be used?

4 Managing your feelings

In our experience, there are few opportunities for you as parents to talk to each other about what it feels like to provide personal and intimate care for your children. This is probably because intimate care for older children and adults is something that is often 'out of view' from the public. Yet it is rarely a neutral subject and it is completely normal for parents to experience all sorts of emotions – sadness, anger, disgust, joy and guilt, to name a few. We have found that allowing space for these feelings, rather than pushing them away, is often what helps parents to make a choice about how they want to interact with and respond to children who need support. If your actions are guided by your values, and your desire to be the kind of parent you want to be in that moment of providing support, then you will be more able to meet your child's needs in a way that helps you both to feel okay.

4.4 Acne, spots and skincare: Helping my child look after their skin

If your skin is clear and healthy looking, it can help you to look good and feel good. When children go through puberty, the changes in hormones can affect their skin by increasing the production of sebum, leading to spots and acne on their face, neck and back. Young people, and the people supporting them, need to know how to look after their skin. Young people who use wheelchairs may also need help to look after their skin, especially if they need help to move regularly to avoid pressure sores, and if they are unable to move themselves out of the sun into the shade.

DEFINITIONS

Skin is the layer of stretchy cells that covers our body. Its job is to hold the body together, stop fluids leaking out, stop germs getting into the body; and help us to sense touch, temperature and pain. We need to look after our skin and make sure it is protected from the sun.

Acne is a long-term skin condition that results from your hair follicles becoming clogged with old skin cells. It usually occurs on the face but can occur on other parts of the body like the neck, back, legs and arms. Acne can be relatively mild and include a few blackheads and pimples, or more extensive and include whiteheads, greasy skin and scarring. Genes are thought to be the main cause of acne, though cleanliness and diet are also thought to play a role. It is usually most prominent in adolescence and reduces as we enter adulthood.

What's the issue?

Acne is not just a physical issue, it also impacts on our psychological and emotional wellbeing. Because it's so visible when on the face, it can undermine people's social confidence and self-esteem. How we look really matters, to ourselves and to other people. We like to look as good as we can when we are in company, and other people will also judge us by our appearance. This is all quite normal and healthy. So when someone experiences acne, even to a small degree, it can lead to anxiety about how they look. And if it is particularly severe or prolonged, then it can lead to social anxiety and avoidance, even depression. It is important to stress that acne is *not* a vanity issue. Nearly everyone cares about how they look to some degree, whereas vanity is an excessive or all-consuming focus on one's appearance.

Finally, it is worth bearing in mind that not everyone has fantastic skin. Very often photographs in magazines are altered and do not represent real life. And every actor wears makeup during filming to change how their skin looks.

> Alice is 13 years old and is a wheelchair user. She needs help to move in and out of her chair and to move her wheelchair. She is going through puberty and has been getting the occasional spot on her face. Alice would like to use makeup but needs a little help with this. She has a lot of moles on her body and needs help to apply suncream.

What can we do?

1 Teach young people why it is important to keep their skin healthy and what helps to keep it healthy

You could do this through social stories or tick lists to help communicate your message clearly.

Looking after your skin is important because it will:

- keep you healthy

- stop you getting spots that might hurt

- look good, and this might help you feel good

To help keep my skin healthy, I can do these things:

- wash my face twice a day

- drink water every day

- exercise every day

- eat a healthy diet so that I get enough vitamins and minerals

- wear suncream.

2 Teach children what's happening when they get spots and what to do

Explain what's happening to them.

- Spots on your face sometimes make it look red and they can hurt.

- They won't last forever.

- Spots happen to young people when they are growing up.

Teach them how to look after their skin when they have spots:

- Use an exfoliator once a week.

- Wash your face twice a day.

- Don't pick your spots

- Go to the doctor if you have lots of spots that hurt, as he/she may be able to give you some cream or medicine to help.

3 Teach young people how to wash their skin and maybe use makeup

Considering the above example, Alice may like to have some help to choose makeup and learn to apply it. She could be supported to get a free makeover in the beauty department of her local store and to make some choices about what to buy. Teenagers who decide to wear makeup may want to learn about how to take their makeup off and how to cleanse, tone and moisturise.

- Cleanse – this helps to take makeup off and remove dirt – use soap and water, or cleansing wipes, or cleanser and cotton wool.

- Tone – this helps to remove residue – use cotton wool to wipe toner over the face.

- Moisturise – this helps keep the skin stretchy and hydrated – put a small amount of moisturiser on your fingertips and massage it into your face.

4 Teach children to protect their skin against the sun

Minimising exposure to sunlight can also help with skincare. While it can be nice to get a light tan, there are also health risks and skin problems that can follow from too much ultraviolet exposure. Some children will need help to learn why it is important to protect their skin from the sun. You can explain that reducing their exposure to sunlight:

- reduces how quickly skin gets wrinkly

- reduces the likelihood of getting skin cancer, which can make you poorly or lead to death.

All people supporting young people will need to know what support they need to keep them safe in the sun. Alice's support workers also need to be vigilant about making sure she can move to the shade if she needs to.

In the summer, if you are spending time outside you need to:

- wear a hat

- wear sunglasses

- wear suncream.

4.5 My son's body odour is getting stronger. What should I do?

Everyone has some level of body odour (often called 'BO') and for the most part we don't notice either our own or other people's. But occasionally body odour becomes stronger and then it can become an issue. BO usually becomes an issue for people when they start puberty and their sweat glands become more active (see definitions box). BO is a problem because it is not (usually) a nice smell and this can have negative effects on social relationships. For instance, people might begin to avoid the person with BO, comment on it negatively or even tease and bully them because of it. Fortunately, BO is not inevitable and there are things we can do to manage and minimise it. The easiest and most effective way to do this is to wash regularly and to use deodorants. But that, of course, is easier said than done.

DEFINITIONS

Body odour (BO) is an unpleasant smell that occurs when body sweat is broken down by bacterial activity. This mostly happens in the armpit area, where we have a cluster of sweat-producing eccrine and apocrine glands. Sweat itself is relatively odourless, though it does contain pheromones that are linked to puberty and sexual behaviour. Human sweat glands become active during puberty, which is why body odour usually becomes an issue when children enter adolescence (though it can occur sooner than this). BO is influenced by what we eat, physical activity levels, drug/alcohol consumption and some medications. Being overweight and some medical conditions (e.g. diabetes) can also increase body odour levels. And finally, males are more likely to have BO than females because, in general, they sweat more.

What's the issue?

When young people enter puberty, they are usually acutely aware of the changes that are occurring in their body and this includes any increased sweating and related BO. As a consequence they are often highly motivated to keep clean and therefore to wash regularly. The cliché of the teenager spending hours in the bathroom is well known.

This is not always the case for children with disabilities. This is because the main driver for managing our BO is social. It is feedback from other people about our cleanliness and/or our desire not to upset other people with our BO that motivates us to wash and keep clean. But if someone isn't very sensitive to, or socially aware of, other people, then they are not going to be particularly responsive to any social feedback they might receive, or worry about what they might think. For children with autistic profiles or general intellectual disabilities, however, this is quite common and this is why BO can be an issue for them. They might not be aware of how they smell to other people, or they might be aware but are just not bothered by it. Either way, the usual motivator of social feedback and a desire to be liked by our peers is not present for these children.

Finally, another situation when BO can be an issue is when a person is physically unable to wash themselves. If they are able to express themselves, they will be able to let you know that they would like to be washed regularly. If their communication isn't clear, we would recommend an assessment of their opinion about what they would like.

> Jack is 15 years old and has an autistic spectrum diagnosis and mild learning disability. He lives with his mum and dad and two younger sisters. Jack was never very keen on keeping clean and having a bath, and when he was younger this was not really an issue. However, since puberty began, his BO has become very noticeable. His sisters regularly complain when they are in the living room together and they don't like to go on car journeys with him either. Jack's parents are also worried that he is being teased by other children and that his BO is stopping him making friends. They would like him to wash more regularly, but in the past it has been such a battle that now he only has a quick shower once a week, sometimes less often. And when he does have a shower, he doesn't wash himself properly, so he often continues to have BO afterwards. He will use deodorants, but usually forgets and doesn't like to be reminded.

 What can we do?

When the usual social motivators are not having much of an effect on your child's inclination to wash themselves, you have two related options (that can be used together):

- Increase their awareness of their BO and how this can affect other people.

- Use other motivators to encourage them to wash and use deodorants.

4.6 How do I help my child learn to use the toilet independently?

Continence is both a health issue and a quality of life issue. Using the toilet independently is important for privacy, dignity and self-esteem. Conversely, not being able to use the toilet independently has significant negative social, financial and health consequences. For example, incontinence can lead to embarrassment, undermine the development of friendships and limit participation in community, educational and recreational activities. Continence pads and nappies need to be bought, worn and disposed of several times a day, every day of the year. Changing a pad takes time and effort and has been linked to health risks for carers, such as diarrhoea and hepatitis. Finally, there is a significant environmental cost as most pads are not biodegradable and need to be incinerated or sent to landfill sites.

DEFINITIONS

Continence is the ability to store urine in the bladder or faeces in the bowel and to expel them voluntarily at socially appropriate times and places. It is common for people with intellectual disabilities to have difficulties with learning to be continent. There are a number of reasons for this – for example, the nature of their intellectual impairment may impact their general learning ability or it may be due to the effects of medication/drugs, or behavioural, dietary and emotional issues.

The average person empties their bladder six times a day at 4–6 hourly intervals. Opening of the bowels is less frequent, usually no more than three times a day and no less than three times a week. Faecal stools should be soft and comfortable to pass. If you feel your child has an unusual pattern for opening their bladder or bowel, or you notice them passing anything unusual, it is best to seek immediate advice from your GP.

In order to support your child's privacy, dignity and health, it is always a good idea to teach them to use the toilet as independently as possible. Even if they will never be fully continent, they can still learn some skills that allow them to be a little bit more independent.

What's the issue?

It is very common that children with intellectual disabilities have difficulties learning to use the toilet independently. This means that until they have learned these skills they will be dependent on other people supporting them with their intimate personal care on a daily basis. They may also have communication difficulties such that they are unable to express clearly their wishes and desires – for example, when they want to use the toilet, if they are feeling uncomfortable or how they feel about other people providing personal care.

Another important reason for improving continence skills is that it reduces the risk of sexual abuse. Sometimes people have their intimate care needs met on a one-to-one basis, and this opens up the possibility (albeit low) that carers can behave sexually inappropriately. Being able to use the toilet independently reduces this possibility.

Teaching your child to use the toilet might feel quite daunting at first, particularly if they have a more severe intellectual disability. In our experience, however, even children with very high support needs can learn to improve their continence skills, even if they don't ever become fully independent.

Jeni is an 8-year-old girl with a severe intellectual disability and autism. She communicates with simple signs and picture cards. She wears continence pads all day but recently she has shown signs that she doesn't like wearing them and she pulls them off when soiled. After discussing the issue with her school, her parents decide it's time to implement a continence programme. Because Jeni doesn't respond well to social praise, her parents decide to use a token board. She gets one token for going to the toilet, one for sitting on the toilet for two minutes and one for washing her hands. When she has three tokens, she can play on a tablet computer for five minutes. And if she urinates in the toilet, she gets a favourite mint sweet. Jeni quickly gets the idea and after two weeks, when she is regularly opening her bladder in the toilet, her parents stop using the sweet as a reinforcer and instead rely on just the tokens, which works just fine.

What can we do?

Improving continence skills is relatively straightforward, but it usually requires some sustained and structured effort. There are now some excellent programmes and resources to help children learn and improve their continence skills. Some of the earliest examples were developed by two American psychologists, Nate Azrin and Richard Foxx in the 1970s (Azrin and Foxx 1989). They showed how a simple five-step process could be used to quickly develop full urinary continence skills. The steps are:

1. Increased fluid intake – give your child a little extra fluid (ideally water) to drink to give them more opportunities to practise using the toilet.

2. Scheduled toileting – prompt your child to sit on the toilet at regular intervals throughout the day.

3. Praise – give them lots of positive feedback when they urinate in the toilet.

4. Positive practice – if they have an accident, encourage them to help you wash themselves and change clothes, and maybe clean up the mess.

5. Communication – use consistent language to prompt them to use the toilet and to communicate when they are going to the toilet or want to go to the toilet.

An example programme to help your child use the toilet independently:

1. Increase fluid: At every meal give Tom an extra cup of water to drink.

2. Scheduled toileting: Take Tom to the toilet three to five times per day, at approximately 60–90-minute intervals. In the toilet, prompt him to take his trousers down and sit on the toilet for up to 30 seconds. When on the toilet, tell Tom, 'You need to do a wee in the toilet', to encourage him to urinate. Keep him on the toilet for three minutes, occasionally reminding him to 'do a wee in the toilet'.

3. Praise: When he urinates in the toilet, say, 'Well done, you've weed in the toilet', and use other positive statements. Help him to get off the toilet and to wash his hands. After leaving the bathroom, you can give him a favourite toy to play with.

4. Positive practice: When Tom has an accident and urinates in his underpants, acknowledge this by saying 'Oh Tom, you've had an accident' and take him to be changed. When in the changing area, encourage him to remove as much of his wet clothing himself as he can, and them to wash and dress to the best of his ability.

5. Communication training: Before each scheduled toileting, say, 'It's time to use the toilet', and then say or sign 'toilet' to Tom. Encourage him to say or sign 'toilet' before taking him to the toilet, and praise him when he does so. Over time you can fade this prompt as he begins to say or sign 'toilet' independently.

This basic programme can be adapted to reflect your child's individual needs. For instance, they might not find verbal praise reinforcing, so instead you could give them a favourite toy or a sticker after they open their bladder. However, if you do this, we recommend only using an extra treat for up to two weeks and to stop using it as soon as you can. The reason for this is that we don't want your child to come to think that using the toilet is all about getting something nice. Instead, we want them to learn to use the toilet to empty their bladder and bowels. We want the positive feelings they will have after emptying their bladder to be the natural reinforcer for using the toilet. So be careful when using additional treats to encourage toilet use, because they can distract the child away from noticing their feelings and inadvertently cause them to become dependent on getting a treat in order to use the toilet.

You can use a similar process for teaching your child to open their bowels on the toilet, though without stage 1 – increased fluid – as this will make no difference to how often they open their bowels.

Finally, be patient. It can take quite a long time (months and even years) for a child to learn to use the toilet, and for long periods it can seem as though no progress is being made. But in our experience every child can improve their continence skills to some degree; it's just a question of sticking with it. To help keep track of your progress, we recommend keeping daily records. Just a quick note on your calendar or even a simple number rating system (1–5, where 1 is 'needs support with every stage' and 5 is 'fully independent') can help you check how things are going.

If you would like any extra support with this, it might be possible to have some help from a school health nurse, or your GP. Sometimes, families can be referred on to specialist intellectual disability services if things are a little more complex.

4.7 What should I do when my son has erections when I change his continence pad?

Having erections during personal and intimate care is actually quite common in young males, particularly when they are starting adolescence. The reasons are more often to do with the general stimulation of the child's genital area caused by the changing process than a sexual interest focused on the carer. Even so, it can still be quite disconcerting when a child's sexual arousal happens so consistently at this time. If this is happening for your child, if you haven't already done so, then it is time to undertake an assessment of his emerging sexuality and put in place processes to support him in this area.

Changing a continence pad will require some level of contact with your son's penis and genital area. This will inevitably provide some level of physiological stimulation that could set off the hormones that lead to an erection. Even something as basic as a change in air temperature around the genitals when a pad is removed can provide enough of a stimulus to set off erectile hormones. It is similar to the observation commonly reported by parents that babies will often urinate when their nappy is removed. It seems that the stimulus of fresh, cooler air tells the child it's time to open their bladder. A further complication is that your child can learn that certain environmental cues mean they are about to be changed in the near future and this can lead to the release of anticipatory erectile-inducing hormones.

What's the issue?

There are two related problems that can arise when your son has erections when he is being changed, one practical and one emotional.

- Practical factors: Changing a pad and cleaning his genital area will be more of a challenge when he has an erection. For instance, it may be harder to move his limbs and body into the positions needed to clean him and it will be more difficult to put on a pad if his erection is full. In addition he is likely to be behaviourally more active if he has an erection because his genital areas will be sensitised to stimulation. This could involve him being generally less cooperative, more agitated, or even frustrated and aggressive. He may also try to masturbate during the changing process when he has access to his genitals. All of these behaviours will make the changing process more difficult.

- Emotional factors: How you feel when your son has an erection while being changed can make the whole process harder. For a start, cleaning up urine and faeces is not a pleasant task. It can be smelly and messy, and it also carries some disease and health implications that need to be managed. These factors will often lead to difficult thoughts and feelings as you engage in the process. While people rarely complain about these issues openly, the negative feelings that typically arise can add to the overall challenge.

In our experience, parents will uniformly say that changing their children's continence pad becomes much harder after they enter puberty. Before adolescence, parents have told us that changing a pad and cleaning their children feels like an extension of caring for them as a baby, but when they start puberty and their bodies take on their adult form (e.g. more muscular and growing pubic hair), the issue becomes more complicated. Even when a parent knows their child will be dependent on others for their intimate care throughout their life, cleaning their genital areas can still be emotionally challenging. Parents just do not expect or indeed want to be providing intimate care for their children once they are no longer children. But this is a reality for some young people and day in, day out their parents show incredible commitment and love when carrying out this task, even though they might feel uncomfortable, disconcerted and upset at the same time.

 ### What can we do?

In terms of what can be done practically, when things are not going well it is a good idea to review the whole process to see if anything can be done differently.

- Can you alter anything about the routine?

- Are any instructions you give him clear and understood?

- How much can he do for himself?

- Can the timing be altered so he is less likely to be sexually stimulated?

Basically, review everything about your changing routine and see if anything can be done differently. When reviewing what we do, it is often a good idea to do it with someone else. Because we are so connected to our own behaviour, it can be difficult to evaluate ourselves objectively. That's why talking it through with someone else can help us stand back from what we are doing and get a new perspective on it. Sometimes as soon as you start to speak with other people, it is obvious what needs to be done. And even if the answer is that there is 'very little' that can really change, at least you know this more certainly.

One area that is always worth investigating is whether your son can help more with his own self-care. It is not uncommon for parents to continue to use the same basic care routine that they developed years earlier when their child was much younger and needed more help. In many ways this makes a lot of sense because when times are busy it takes minimal mental effort to follow a familiar routine, but this can mean that the potential for your child to do more of his own self-care is overlooked. Again, it can help to discuss this with someone else, perhaps a developmental psychologist, who can give you some ideas about how to help your child learn more self-care skills. This can take time, literally years; but once he has the skills, he has them for life. It also has the positive side effect of giving him something else to do during the changing process and this can reduce how sexually aroused he becomes.

It is also important to recognise the emotional challenge the whole process can represent for you. Noticing and being aware of how you feel as you change your son's pad and support his sexuality is an important first step towards acceptance. There is a growing body of research showing that acceptance of our thoughts and feelings is vital for our wellbeing as it creates the space to behave in line with our underlying values. Acceptance isn't about giving up or passively tolerating what is happening to us. If you can change something that is causing you difficulties, then do so. But if what you are doing can't be changed, at least in the short term, then your best option is to accept it.

Psychological acceptance is about being open to all your thoughts, feelings and bodily sensations, the good and the bad. This isn't as straightforward as you might think as we naturally want to shy away from negative experiences rather than accept them. So why bother trying to accept negative thoughts and feelings rather then avoid or get rid of them? The reason is that in fact we have very little control over what we think and feel and this means we are unlikely to have much success trying to control or avoid them. Rather than wasting time trying not to have certain negative thoughts and feelings, accepting them instead allows us to stay focused on what really matters to us and for our behaviour to be guided by our values rather than how we might be feeling or what we might be thinking. For instance, it might be important to you to be a loving parent and in the service of this value you lovingly change your child's pad and manage any sexualised behaviour even when you have thoughts and feelings that might be encouraging you to do the opposite.

4.8 My daughter is growing pubic hair, what should I do?

As girls go through puberty, the hair on their legs starts to grow and may become thicker. Girls also start to grow hair under their arms and in their pubic area. Deciding what to do with extra hair, especially pubic hair, is usually a cultural and religious choice. Many girls and women decide to remove their underarm hair because it helps with hygiene and reducing body odour. Many decide also to remove their leg hair and pubic hair, and some also decide to remove hair from parts of their eyebrows and upper lip (if it becomes darker).

Young people often wonder when to start removing extra hair. This is a personal choice, but it is okay to start when hair first appears on their underarms, legs and pubic area. Girls and women have choices about how to remove hair: the most common is to shave it; some also wax or use hair removal cream.

What's the issue?

Amy's Mum is considering whether her daughter is ready to make a decision about removing her pubic hair, as well as whether she can learn the skills to manage this safely. Learning the skills to manage hair removal can be tricky for all young women. For girls and young women with disabilities, there might be some extra reasons why this is tricky. For example, young women with cerebral palsy may feel scared of learning to shave independently using a razor because of lack of control or grip with their hands. If young people are completely physically dependent on help from others, they may feel embarrassed to ask for help with it, especially in relation to pubic hair.

Young women with autism may have particular sensory sensitivities that make it hard for them to use shaving cream or to tolerate the feeling of a razor or waxing. Some young women with intellectual disabilities may find it hard to make independent choices about hair removal and parents might be in a position of making the decision for them. It can then be difficult for carers to know whether to go ahead with this intimate task if it is a cultural preference rather than a necessary task.

What can we do?

1 Provide information about shaving/ hair removal and what to do

Most girls learn to shave their extra hair by watching their parent or carer and through parents giving verbal instructions. Children with disabilities may need some extra information to help them understand what is happening and what to do. This might be in the form of a social story and/or tick list.

2 Help your child make choices based on sensory preferences

Help your daughter make some choices based on her sensory preferences. Some young women may be able to choose their preferred shaving gel or cream based on scent and texture. Some may be able to tolerate the strong smell and sensation of hair removal cream, but will require a skin patch test first to ensure they do not have a reaction to it. Some may prefer to wax. This is obviously more painful and some young women may not be able to tolerate the temperature of the wax. However, it means that they won't have to worry about shaving frequently.

3 Think about safety

Think about what kind of razor your daughter might need in order to avoid nicks and cuts. A wide-handled razor may be easier to grip. The more substantial razors, as opposed to the cheaper disposable ones, can sometimes be safer. Some young women prefer to use an electric razor, which can be safer but does not give as close a shave as an ordinary one. Teach your daughter how often to change her razor and how to dispose of it safely.

4 Who should help your daughter with shaving?

Most parents/carers expect to help their daughter with learning how to remove body hair, but many do not anticipate having to help for long. When you have a child who may be dependent on some kind of support for physical tasks for the long-term future, it can be helpful to have discussions with her about who she feels comfortable asking for help. Many women have their pubic hair (bikini line) and/or legs waxed by someone outside the family at a beauty salon. This might be your daughter's preference too. She might feel more comfortable asking a personal assistant to help her. However, these are often conversations that get avoided because they can be embarrassing or uncomfortable. Using an intimate care plan can be a way of structuring the conversation and documenting your daughter's choices. It may also help to focus on the development of independence skills in relation to shaving or hair removal.

Learning how to shave

When girls grow up, they start to grow hair under their arms, on their legs and between their legs on their private parts. Some girls and women shave some of their hair. It is up to them what they decide to shave. Most women shave the hair under their arms. Younger children do not need to shave.

When women shave, they usually do it in the shower. They put some cream or soap on the hair under their arms. They use a special razor and shave the hair. Then they rinse off the soap and hair with water. Razors are very sharp and need to be kept safely away from children. When women have finished shaving, they rinse off the razor and put it away.

4.9 My son is growing facial hair, what should I do?

Growing facial hair is usually a sign your son is in the later stages of puberty. Boys typically start developing facial hair at around 14–16 years of age, though it can start earlier. Human biological development is not a rigid or fixed process and there can be a lot of variation from one child to the next. The development of facial hair continues for a number of years and males are usually well into their 20s before they can grow a full beard.

Interestingly, facial hair has often been seen as a sign of wisdom, virility and manhood. While beards and moustaches come in and out of fashion in many developed countries, they continue to be important symbols for many communities in the UK and around the world. Facial hair can also have religious significance, with some religions (e.g. Sikhism) expecting their followers to grow beards. Therefore, for some young males it will be important to grow a moustache or beard as part of their adult identity, and others will want to shave off any facial hair.

What's the issue?

Children can react in a number of ways to growing facial hair. Some children like growing facial hair as it signifies they are moving into adulthood or because it has a positive cultural/religious value. Other children will hardly notice it and not particularly care either way.

At the other end of the spectrum, a small minority can become quite upset by their facial hair. For these children, the issue is often (though not always) related to changes in their body and anxiety about what it means to become an adult. This is quite natural, of course, and part of the wider issue of what puberty means for the child. Supporting your child to understand what is happening with his body as it changes during puberty will help him cope with it more effectively.

A secondary issue related to growing facial hair is shaving. This is often a bigger issue than growing facial hair in the first place. Although it is often taken for granted, shaving actually involves quite a complex set of motor actions, and it also takes quite a bit of motivation to even start the process. Helping children learn the skills to shave will make the task easier. This will make the whole process less arduous, which means it will require less motivation.

 What can we do?

The first step is to be clear what facial hair means for your child and for you. Because they will see facial hair on men and learn about it in school as something that happens when boys grow up, most children will understand that it is something that will happen when they become an adult. But sometimes this information isn't fully understood, so it is always a good idea to check out your child's understanding about facial hair. When this information is presented in a relaxed and straightforward way, they will learn that it is a natural part of growing up into a man and nothing to be worried about.

If growing a beard has cultural or religious significance, then help your son understand this too so he can be proud of any facial hair he has.

The next major issue is shaving and how to do it. It is quite common for parents to shave their children's facial hair, particularly when they are younger or just learning. This has the initial advantage of helping your child to be neatly clean-shaven without any cuts or nicks, and it's usually quicker too. The downside is that your child won't learn to shave himself as long as you are doing it. So we would recommend a compromise, whereby you gradually help your child to do more and more himself so he can be as independent as possible.

Teaching your child to shave might seem a little daunting at first, but any complex behaviour like shaving can be broken down into smaller steps that can be mastered one at a time. One way to do this is with what's called a task analysis. This involves breaking down the skill you want your child to learn and then teaching them each step sequentially – as with the five-step programme to teach urinary continence described earlier. For shaving with a manual razor this might look like the list below:

1. Find your razor and soap/foam.

2. Check the razor is not damaged.

3. Fill up the sink with some water.

4. Lather up some soap or squirt some shaving foam onto your hand.

5. Put the soap/foam onto your bearded area.

6. Pick up the razor and with a slow, careful, single stroke pull the razor down over one cheek.

7. Wash the razor in the sink.

8. Repeat steps 6 and 7 until your face has been shaved.

9. Empty the sink.

10. Wash your face in clean water and dry yourself with a towel.

This example is only meant as a guide for what you might do. It could be simpler or more complex, depending on what your son needs helps with. The general principle is for your son to do as much as possible himself. It might take several months or even longer, but once he has mastered the skill, he will be able to do it for the rest of his life.

The final point to consider is motivation. It is quite common for children and young adolescents to be uninterested in washing and grooming in general. As they grow older and become interested in the opposite sex, this can change, but not always. Washing, after all, takes time and effort and can be a bit of a chore. If this is the case, you might need to think about using some additional motivation – for instance, insisting that they are clean and well groomed before going out to a club or the cinema or doing something else they enjoy. Of course you want them to do these things, so you can offer to help them if needed. The idea is to give them a bit of extra motivation to wash and shave, rather than to have a battle about it. If you find yourself in a battle, that indicates that the task is a bit too challenging for your son at that point in time. To reduce your battles, try asking for something that they will feel is relatively easy to do. Then, when this is established, you can say, 'Well done, you are doing this so well, I'd like you to do this little bit extra too', and then specify a small additional task.

4.10 How do I teach my daughter to use sanitary pads?

Menstruation, sometimes called a 'period', is when blood comes out of a woman's vagina for a few days every month. It happens when the egg released by the woman's body is not fertilised, and hormones break down the lining of the womb, which then leaves the body as a period. After the period, hormones help to thicken the womb lining to prepare for another egg to be released. Menstruation is an ordinary, healthy part of growing up, and can be seen as a stepping stone to adulthood.

For some parents/carers of daughters with intellectual disabilities, menstruation can be seen as challenge because they worry about whether their daughter has the ability to understand what's happening, or the physical abilities to manage it independently and hygienically. Many parents are concerned about how their daughter will tolerate a sanitary pad. For some parents, it can feel very uncomfortable to have to help with managing what is usually a very private event.

Michelle McCarthy (2010) has carried out a lot of research with women with intellectual disabilities, and has found that, even in the 21st century, women with intellectual disabilities are not always prepared for the start of their periods and are not sure what the change to their bodies means. We think this is probably because it is an area that causes a lot of worry, as well as confusion about how best to support young women. However, we know that when young women are supported to understand and manage their periods, it can have a positive impact on how they feel about themselves and their bodies. It can also help to keep them safe, as it means that they may not have to rely on others to provide personal care for them.

What's the issue?

For most young women with intellectual disabilities, menstruation will follow the same process as for women without intellectual disabilities. However, some young women with neurological differences can start puberty early, and so their periods could also start earlier than expected (the average age is 12 for young women without neurological differences). Some medications can affect menstrual cycles, and menstrual problems can occur for young women who have thyroid problems, which is a common problem for women with Down's syndrome.

Hayley is 10 years old, her Mum has noticed that her body has been changing and she started to go through puberty quite early. Hayley is a very active child and rarely sits still. She finds it difficult to concentrate and listen. She communicates using some signing and using photographs. Her Mum is sure that she will start her periods early but she does not know how to have the 'talk' with Hayley, as she thinks she would find it really hard to understand. Hayley's Mum is wondering whether to get her used to sanitary pads early or just address the issue when it happens. She is worried that it could be messy and embarrassing for Hayley if she doesn't tolerate having sanitary pads in her underwear. Hayley's mother might have had thoughts or hopes about what it might be like to talk to her daughter about menstruation, as for some women this can be considered an important and special time. It would be understandable if Hayley's mum felt a mixture of emotions about not being able to have the 'talk'; maybe sadness or worry. However, she is still considering how she can have the talk in a different way, to support her daughter in preparing for her period, and to be as autonomous as possible.

What can we do?

1 Preparation: Understanding the life cycle

It can be helpful to explain to girls and young women that starting periods is part of what happens to them over the life cycle; that is, it is what happens to girls as they grow up. We think it is important that girls learn that, as they become adults, there will be changes to their body, including growing breasts and wearing a bra, growing hair under their arms and between their legs, and having blood come out of their vagina for a few days a month. It is important to let young women know that this happens to all women and that they are not ill or dying.

It is possible that the school may help children to understand these concepts. If you wanted to help your child understand at home, you could use pictures or photographs to show the life cycle. You could start to name the changes that have already happened for your daughter and let her know what might happen next.

2 Practicalities and hygiene

PADS, TAMPONS AND CONTINENCE PADS

Young women with intellectual disabilities should be given the same opportunities to choose products that are comfortable for them. If your child is physically able to manage to insert a tampon, and to learn how to do this, then this should be considered as an option, and it could be the preferred option for women who find it difficult to manage and dispose of pads hygienically. However, we also need to consider how to support a young woman in the least intrusive way possible.

For example, if your daughter can change her own knickers, then you could help by placing the pad into the knickers and allowing her to change herself. Later, her skills in changing the pads whilst keeping her knickers on could be developed.

If your child is incontinent and already wears continence pads, it is possible to additionally use a sanitary pad on top of the pad, as it will be more effective in absorbing blood, and also acts as a visual cue to your child, to let her know that something different is happening.

You could consider using aprons and gloves in order to manage infection control.

Consider with your child who they would like or not like to help them with their periods.

3 Communication

It will be important to let your child know through symbols and objects that she is menstruating and so some parts of her routine will be different. If you use a visual timetable or planner with your child, you could start to introduce her to the symbols that you will use for menstruation and for 'changing'. You could let her know where you keep the sanitary pads. It can be helpful to use a social story to show her what to do to change her pad and how to dispose of it.

If this is too complex and your daughter needs support from you to do this for her, it is important to let her know what is happening by commenting on what you are doing, and using symbols to support this. You should ensure that your daughter can access a symbol for pain, in order to be able to let you know if she is experiencing abdominal cramps or other pain.

Some young people will need reminders and support to change their pads regularly. You could help by setting a regular alarm on your child's watch, or asking teaching staff to prompt her and support her at the beginning of break times during the school day.

Is it possible to stop my child's periods altogether?

In certain circumstances, women with intellectual disabilities are prescribed oral contraceptives or the depo-provera injection (a birth control method) in order to totally stop their periods. However, decisions need to be considered in each person's best interests, as this is not without possible adverse consequences (Albanese and Hopper 2007) including the development of osteoporosis with long-term use. Please discuss with your child's school health nurse, GP or paediatrician if you would like to find out further information.

Hayley's mum started by showing her daughter the changes that had already happened to her body by looking at photographs of her from a baby to now. She prepared her daughter for the next stage of development by talking to her about what would happen next. She started to show her daughter where she kept the sanitary pads and showed her how she put them into her knickers. She used one of the resources mentioned below (I change my pad) to show her what might happen.

Even though Hayley did not seem to understand what her mum was showing her, when the time came and her periods started, the booklet and the process of changing her pad was a little familiar. Her mum had started using a calendar for Hayley, and every morning they looked at the calendar to see if it was a school day or a home day. Now, her mum started adding a symbol for 'pad change' and let Hayley know when it was a day she had to remember to change her pads. At school there was a plan in place for two members of staff to help her with changing her pad at every break time. She carried a social story with photographs in her pocket. Staff at school encouraged Hayley to take responsibility for removing her pad and her Mum helped her to practise this at home.

4.11 What should I do about wet dreams, soiled pyjamas and bedding?

Having an orgasm and ejaculating semen while asleep is a common occurrence for adolescent boys. This is often called a 'wet dream' as the semen will make either pyjamas or the bedding wet. When this happens the semen will leave a residue that will mean either the pyjamas or bedding will need to be washed. It is less well known that adolescent females can also have an orgasm while sleeping, but because no semen is ejaculated there is no evidence for this in the morning. This means it will often go unnoticed.

Adolescents have orgasms while asleep when they have an erotic dream (which is basically a form of thinking) that leads them to become sexually aroused. This is not surprising as human beings become sexually aroused when we think about erotic events whether we are awake or asleep. It's not clear why we think about sex while we are asleep. It may be that we are dreaming about things that have happened or that we would like to happen. Whatever the reason for erotic dreams, they are a common human experience, particularly for adolescents.

What's the issue?

Having an orgasm while asleep presents the same three main issues for both disabled and non-disabled young people – hygiene, embarrassment and anxiety.

What can we do?

Let's look at them one at a time:

1. Hygiene: After having a wet dream it is important to wash clothing and bedding after ejaculating onto it. Your child might not always be aware he has had a wet dream and so might not be aware of the need to change pyjamas and/or bedding. Or he might know he has had a wet dream, but still not be motivated to wash. Regularly washing and keeping clean is not always a priority for young people, which means they often need some extra encouragement from parents and carers. This is quite

natural and getting into a regular routine for washing is often the best way to help youngsters stay clean and hygienic (see Section 4.2).

2. Embarrassment: The young person may be aware he has ejaculated and be embarrassed that his parents or carers know what has happened. This is quite common, particularly as it is usually parents and carers who will do the household washing, including bedding and pyjamas. If you notice bedclothes or pyjamas are stained with dried semen, it is probably best not to comment on this. It's a natural event for young people and there is no need to draw attention to it unless your child wants to know about it or if it is creating an issue. If your child asks you about it, it will be helpful to him to explain what has happened and that it is perfectly normal. You might also use the opportunity to encourage him to put his clothing in the wash basket!

3. Anxiety: Sometimes children can become anxious and worried about ejaculating semen and having wet dreams. When this happens, spend a bit of time finding out why they are worried by checking out what they think is happening. In our experience, the worry is usually related to fears there is something wrong with them. If this is the case, then their anxieties can usually be dealt with by simply explaining what is happening and that it is all perfectly normal.

Resources

Family Planning Association (2014) *Periods: What You Need to Know.* London: FPA.

Rees, M., Carter, C. and Myers, L. (2008) *Periods – A Practical Guide.* Sedbergh: Me-and-Us Ltd.

Rees, M., Carter, C. and Myers, L. (2008) *I Change My Pad.* Sedbergh: Me-and-Us Ltd.

The Elfrida Society. *Help! I've Started My Periods.* Available at www.easyhealth.org.uk/listing/periods-(leaflets), accessed 4 April 2016.

Chapter 5

BEHAVIOUR

This chapter presents questions that parents often ask about their children's behaviour during puberty. It looks at some of the more common problems that arise and what can be done about them.

5.1 My son keeps talking about women's bodies. What can I do?

People love to talk, and in general we talk about things we are interested in. If your son is talking about women's bodies, it is probably because he is showing a sexual interest in women. This is entirely natural and most adolescent boys talk with each other about women's bodies and sex. Likewise, it is common for young females to talk about male bodies and sex.

DEFINITIONS

People with a heterosexual orientation usually talk about the bodies of the opposite sex for erotic reasons. This type of talk will typically focus on parts of the body associated with sex – like breasts, the penis, buttocks or the vagina, but not always. The reason for this is that human beings can find any part of the body sexually attractive. For example, it is quite common for people to find hands, feet, ears and even noses sexually attractive.

What's the issue?

Talking about people's bodies or sex in general is quite natural and normal. The issue is that this should be at the right time and place, and most importantly it should be done respectfully.

One thing to consider, however, is that just because someone talks about sex (or bodies), that doesn't necessarily mean they are actually showing a sexual interest. Sometimes people talk about sex to get a reaction out of others and not because they are sexually aroused or focused. For example, we have worked with children who have said things to female teachers like 'I want to sex you' or 'You've got big tits'. Understandably, the teachers were unsettled by these statements and felt the boys were being sexually provocative. People will naturally react when they hear things like this, because sex is a sensitive topic in Western societies. But on these occasions the children's language was not an expression of sexual desire or interest, but served to get the teachers attention – and it was very effective at achieving this. So the key question to ask is: why is the child or young person saying what they are saying? Depending on their reasons, different responses will be required.

What can we do?

The first thing to do is find out why your child is talking about other people's bodies. Are they showing a genuine sexual interest or are they more interested in the effect of what they are saying? If you aren't sure, you can ask other people to observe what is happening and see what they say. To understand someone's behaviour, we need to look at the consequences to which it leads. Observe what happens after the behaviour has occurred and this will give you the best idea of why your child is saying what they say.

If it turns out that they are expressing a sexual interest, this suggests they would benefit from some basic sex education. This will help them understand the thoughts and feelings they are having. It will also give them guidance about how to behave towards themselves and other people. Or you could have a chat with them about what is interesting them and answer any questions they might have.

Talking about sex or bodies for social reasons is actually very common, particularly amongst children and adolescents. Young children, for instance, will often say 'bum' or 'willy' because they know they shouldn't or to make a joke with friends. Talking about sex in public is a taboo issue in Western societies, so any mention will generate a social reaction. If your child is talking about sex or people's bodies to get a social reaction, it is worth considering what social reaction they are after as this will be a guide for how to respond.

- If they want to get your attention, the best option is to ignore any references to sex and only respond to them when they have begun to talk about something else. Telling them off for sex talk is unlikely to be effective as it will just provide more attention, which is what they are after.

- If they want you to stop asking them to do something (called *demand avoidance*), the best thing to do is ignore what they are saying and maintain your request until they comply. It might seem a little odd, but actually making sexually explicit statements is a very good way of avoiding demands because it unsettles and distracts the person making the request.

- Be aware that the reasons for sex talk can vary over time, maybe even in the same day. Sometimes it can be about a genuine interest in sex, at other times it can be about getting social attention and or avoiding/delaying a demand. This means a single response is unlikely to be effective. Instead you will have to decide what the reason is for their sex talk each time it occurs and then respond accordingly.

Paul is 15 years old and has a moderate intellectual disability. In the last three months he has begun to talk about women's bodies, particularly his teachers' bottoms and breasts. His teachers are a little upset by his behaviour and a meeting is called by his school. At the meeting it is agreed that Paul would benefit from some additional education around sex and relationships. But even after he has completed an individually tailored programme, he continues to make sexually explicit statements to his teachers. The initial assumption is that he hasn't understood the sex education training programme, until a teaching assistant observes that he usually engages in sex talk during transitions he doesn't want to do. This helps the school understand that part of the reason Paul was talking about sex was to delay an unwanted transition.

5.2 My son keeps trying to masturbate, but doesn't know how: What can I do?

Masturbation is quite normal and it does not have any negative effects on the body (as long as it isn't excessive). For many young people with intellectual disabilities it is the only form of sexual behaviour freely available to them, as they may not have the capacity to consent to sexual activity with another person. However, the process of knowing about masturbation and all of the social rules that go with it may be different for them compared to their mainstream peers.

DEFINITIONS

Masturbation means touching your own body (genitals) for sexual pleasure and to reach orgasm, usually with your hand but sometimes with objects. It is healthy and natural if you are in the right place, it does not cause emotional or physical harm, and it is usually the first sexual experience that young people have. It is common from pre-adolescent age (10 years upwards) and this may be the same for young people with intellectual disabilities, whose bodies are developing in the same way, even if emotionally and socially they are at a younger developmental age.

What's the issue?

The two most common questions we are asked in relation to masturbation are about how to do it and where to do it. When young people with intellectual disabilities are learning about their bodies they often don't know how to stimulate themselves or where they should go to do it in private.

The main reasons young people with more severe intellectual disabilities masturbate in public is they either do not know the social rules about sexual behaviour in public or they are not particularly sensitive to other people's reactions.

If their public masturbation is due to a lack of social understanding, they need to be taught the rules around public displays of sexual behaviour as quickly as possible. If this is not possible (or will take a long period of time), then your child's dignity and privacy will need to be protected by you intervening to stop your child behaving in this way or by removing them from the public setting.

Often young people with intellectual disabilities are told to go to their bedrooms to masturbate. This is an important message to give, because really their bedroom is the only private place they have. However, this message alone might not be enough to stop the behaviour happening in public. This is because when masturbation occurs outside of the bedroom, it is usually because the young person is sexually aroused by visual stimulation (like a person), which is not available to them in their bedroom. In contrast, young people without intellectual disabilities often have the opportunity and ability to access and use visual stimulation (like pictures of women/men in magazines or on the Internet) in private and hide this away from parents. A lack of sexually stimulating material might be a reason why young people with intellectual disabilities struggle to know that they can masturbate in private in their bedroom.

Sometimes young men start to explore masturbation but do not know how to do it 'successfully'. This raises some difficult questions, such as should you teach your child to masturbate, and if so how?

> Michael is 13 years old. He has Down's syndrome, severe intellectual disability and communicates using non-verbal means including signing, pointing and facial expression. He has recently started to get erections in public and has started rubbing his penis on the carpet. He has started to touch his penis in public but does not seems to know how to masturbate. His family and teachers have been asking him to go to his bedroom or have been using distraction as a way of managing, but they feel that if he knew how to masturbate he would be less frustrated and they could schedule in time for him to do this in private. They have tried teaching him about masturbation by talking to him and using line drawings, but he finds it difficult to pay attention and doesn't seem to be relating the pictures to his own body.

What's happening to Michael?

Michael is going through an ordinary stage of adolescent development and is naturally curious about his body and sexual pleasure. He has limited social awareness around what he is doing, he is not able to make the links between his behaviour and future consequences (e.g. being arrested), he may be less able to understand how it impacts on other people and he has not had an opportunity to find out about masturbation with a peer group or through social media/television, etc.

Michael's family and teachers have made a good start in teaching him about masturbation. As the messages have not had the impact required, they need to think about how to change their way of communicating with Michael and move on to the next step – from talking about it to showing him what to do.

PLEASE NOTE: Under the Sexual Offences Act (2003) it is illegal for care workers to involve people with intellectual disabilities in any kind of sexual behaviour; therefore, it is very important to note that the modelling of masturbation needs to be done using dolls or models and not in real life.

As Michael's school and family have found that line drawings and social stories have not been enough to teach him the skills he needs to masturbate successfully, the next step might be to use the recommended educational video and/or anatomically correct dolls. At this stage we would advise calling a multiagency meeting to discuss Michael's needs and plan how to implement a direct training programme.

 What can we do?

1 Start a basic sex and relationships programme with your child

This is a good first step, which will help them learn how to understand their sexuality and the social rules about how to express it in public. There are guidelines for young people with mild intellectual disabilities such as the 'Puberty and Sexuality' pack (Leeds Nursing, 2009).

2 If your child has more severe intellectual disabilities, they are likely to need more direct support managing their masturbation behaviour

Depending on the level of your child's communication and understanding, there are a number of resources available that you can use, such as:

- Written word: Use social stories or books, such as *Things Tom Likes* (Reynolds 2014), or *Taking Care of Myself* (Wrobel 2003).

- Verbal descriptions/videos: Use 'Jason's Private World' or 'Kylie's Private World' DVDs.[1]

- Line drawings: Use the 'Puberty and Sexuality' pack (Leeds Nursing 2009).[2]

- Models: Use anatomically correct dolls and condom demonstrators (ejaculating).[3]

3 Agree a contract around the work and a plan for teaching

Michael's family and tutor at school could set up a contract and agreed plan for teaching masturbation.

4 Teach the rules of privacy and consider a schedule

At the same time as teaching 'how to do' masturbation, Michael's parents and carers need to consistently teach him about the concepts of public and private. He needs to know that masturbation is not allowed at school at all (because it is a public place), but it is okay at home in his bedroom.

Consider scheduling in private time for him to be alone.

5 Prevention of risks

If your child is unlikely ever to learn the appropriate social rules around masturbation, then they will need support and supervision to ensure their dignity and privacy is maintained in public places. The risk should be continually assessed so that the least restrictive option is used for support.

---

1   Available at www.lifesupportproductions.co.uk/jpwdvd.php
2   Available at www.leeds.gov.uk/docs/Puberty-and-Sexuality-Pack-Session1-4.pdf
3   Available at www.bodysense.org.uk/models.shtml

5.3 My daughter keeps masturbating in public – rubbing herself against things – what can I do?

Female masturbation – stimulating the genitals – is generally considered a safe form of sexual expression for young women, and may be the only form of sexual expression for some women with intellectual disabilities (McCarthy 1999). It is considered to have a positive impact on mood (releasing endorphins), can provide pain relief and is risk free in relation to pregnancy or sexually transmitted infections. As young women with intellectual disabilities grow physically and develop hormonally through puberty and beyond, they may struggle to understand what's happening to their bodies and why they feel different. There may be a new interest in sexual feelings and masturbation, which is completely normal, and at the same time they may not be aware of the social rules associated with this private behaviour.

Challenges might come up for you if:

- your daughter continues to masturbate during menstruation

- your daughter uses objects that lead to soreness or bruising

- your daughter is not aware of appropriate times and places to masturbate.

Jess is 12 and has started showing a sexual interest in her body. She has started using objects to masturbate and has made her genitals sore. She frequently masturbates in public and her family are finding it embarrassing. They are worried about other people's reactions and her vulnerability.

What's the issue?

Jess's parents are understandably feeling uncomfortable and embarrassed by their daughter's public masturbation. Masturbation is usually such a hidden and private behaviour and, when done in public, it compromises Jess' relationships and impacts on her right to dignity. It is likely that other children or adults might avoid her because they too feel embarrassed to see the behaviour. Jess is also beginning to use objects that are making her sore and therefore impacting on her health – probably because she is unaware of what she could use that would be safer and still feel nice.

What can we do?

WARNING SIGNS: Should you have any concerns that a child's behaviour is outside of what you would expect for their age, please take responsibility for following this up as a child protection concern with a health professional or educational professional. This might include a young child masturbating or a child suddenly starting to masturbate in public. These can be signs of sexual abuse.[4]

1 Teach the concepts of public and private

Jess's parents and carers needs to teach her consistently about the concepts of public and private. Instead of telling Jess 'not here', they need to let her know where she can masturbate, for example, 'that's okay in your bedroom'.

---

4   The NSPCC website has further information on signs of abuse (see www.nspcc.org.uk/preventing-abuse/keeping-children-safe/healthy-sexual-behaviour-children-young-people).

Usually, we teach children that private means in your bedroom with your door shut. In our work with schools we have agreed that all of school is a public place. If we were to allow children to masturbate in the bathrooms at school, this might be a confusing message since it would not be okay for them to do it in other public toilets.

Jess's parents/carers can use additional ways of communicating the concept of public and private. For example, they may need to take symbols with them when they go out in the community, and her school would benefit from having a copy of them to reinforce this teaching.

2 Teach when and how – create opportunities for your daughter to access her body

Jess may benefit from knowing when she can masturbate as well as where. For example, she may need a social story that sets out that it is okay for her to touch her private parts when she is at home, in her bedroom on her own, using her hands or objects that do not hurt, like a pillow.

You may want to allow your daughter time to have access to her body if she usually wears continence pads or needs help to remove clothing. Some young women like to masturbate at bath time, because this is the only time they have access to their body. Allowing privacy during this time depends on safety.

Some parents/carers find that young women who continue to masturbate during menstruation cannot manage the hygiene aspect of this and may end up with blood on their hands/clothes/bedding. You may need to decide whether you can teach your daughter to manage the hygiene aspect, or whether you can teach her to choose not to masturbate on a period day. You may want to consider hormonal interventions such as the contraceptive pill to stop menstruation. This final option should be done with the young person's consent, or discussed as a best interests decision with her GP if necessary.

3 Developing alternative ways of spending time or communicating needs

Analysing masturbation as a behaviour just like any other behaviour is sometimes required. In our experience, young people can masturbate to relieve boredom, especially if the activities or lessons they are in are too easy, too difficult or simply not motivating enough for them.

As with any other behaviour, it is important to analyse what's going on for the young person just beforehand, during and after. Jess's parents might need to consider whether she has learnt that if she masturbates in public she gets taken home quickly (and therefore avoids a boring shopping trip). Her behaviour may increase the opportunities for social interaction, as people may start talking to her and telling her to stop. Jess may be masturbating as a way of coping with feeling overwhelmed in busier places. There are lots of different possibilities and her parents could start by keeping a behaviour log for a few days, to discuss with a health professional.

4 What to do if it keeps happening

If the prevention strategies have not yet been effective and your daughter is masturbating in public, you may need to disrupt the behaviour and remind your daughter of the rules (she can masturbate at home in her bedroom in private, not now). You may need to provide her with an alternative activity, and possibly one that involves her hands and her body in a different way – for example, carrying an object to the trolley if you are in the supermarket. If she consistently masturbates at the same time of day, you could try scheduling in private time for her during that time slot. You could also try rewarding her for not masturbating in public (for following her social story). Rewards that are motivating for her will be important – this could be anything from extra time on technology to access to a toy she loves or extra time playing with you.

5.4 My child touches other people inappropriately, what can I do?

During adolescence, sexual urges and feelings may naturally come to the forefront, including an urge to touch, flirt and explore another person's body in an intimate way. Young people are often able to have opportunities for touch that is appropriate and non-sexual, and you may notice that, depending on cultural expectations, touch increases between adolescents – often hugging, holding hands, bumping shoulders, high fives, and so on.

DEFINITIONS

Touch is an important part of human relationships. It is part of our non-verbal communication and something we do with each other without being explicit about the social rules. It helps to build social bonds, and to communicate emotion. Think about how a baby is rocked to sleep, how a parent holds a child's hand, how you can offer sympathy and support with a touch on the shoulder, gratitude by a shake of the hand.

As we go through adolescence and young adulthood, touch becomes sexual with certain people and we begin to have greater intimacy and connection to those we choose to be sexual with. We start to feel that we want to touch and explore the bodies of those we are attracted to. For young people with intellectual disabilities there may be difficulties in understanding the social and sexual rules around touch. There may be difficulties in making sense of and understanding their feelings and urges, and with resisting the urge to touch other people. It may be that the environment young people are in unwittingly limits their opportunities for touch and connection. For example, a wheelchair may be a physical barrier to touch and it may be that a physically disabled young person therefore has fewer opportunities to be physically close to their friends or peers.

Children and young people need to have opportunities for the good things that come with ordinary human touch, as well as knowledge and understanding around the rules of sexual and non-sexual touch. This is what will help keep them safe – to know when and where it is okay for their bodies to be touched, as well as when and where it is okay to touch other people.

> Ben is 15 years old and has diagnoses of autism and severe intellectual disability. Ben's family have started to worry about taking Ben out in the community because he has started to approach women and touch their breasts. He has started to do this at school with some of the teaching assistants and to some of the other students. Some of Ben's support staff have commented that this makes them so uncomfortable they do not think they can provide care for Ben any longer.

What's the issue?

Your child may be experiencing ordinary sexual feelings and urges to explore and touch other people's bodies. On one level this is entirely normal and healthy; it is just that this desire needs to be expressed in socially appropriate ways.

Children who are less socially aware of the consequences of touching other people will need extra support to ensure they understand the socially acceptable ways of behaving sexually in public. It is worth bearing in mind that children can touch other people for a number of reasons, not just sexual ones. For instance, sometimes children will touch other people for the social reaction that follows. In the example of Ben above, the people around him may be unwittingly keeping the behaviour (touching) going because Ben gains a 'big' reaction from those around him, which he enjoys.

What can we do?

1 The environment

Think about the general environment your child is in, at home and school or college. How does the physical environment allow opportunities for safe non-sexual touch? Do they have opportunities for physical and/or sensory play, swimming, clapping games, chasing, hugs? It might be helpful to think about how they can have more opportunities for non-sexual touch in their everyday activities.

2 Teach the difference between public and private

Your child would benefit from education about the concepts of public vs private places and parts of the body. 'Public' means somewhere where there is more than one person. Private means a place where someone is on their own and cannot be seen. Sometimes it is necessary to add that somewhere becomes private when the door is shut. Children often need repeated opportunities to learn the rule that it is not okay to touch other people's private parts. This is because our bodies are private, and it could upset and embarrass other people if you touch them.

You can use pictures of public and private places and parts of the body to help teach these concepts. In addition, it may be helpful for a carer to show which parts of the body are not private by placing green stickers on their body or on a doll to represent places it is okay to touch.

3 Teach about appropriate non-sexual touch – who can you touch, where, and when?

In addition to teaching children what *not* to do, it is important to tell your child what they can do. Your child needs to know how touch might differ depending on the nature of the relationship. For example, Ben could be taught that 'front hugs' or bear hugs are for Mum and Dad only. Side hugs, that is, your arm around someone's shoulders, are for friends. High fives are for friends. We might shake someone's hands if we are introducing ourselves or saying goodbye.

Ben needs to know that it is okay to touch his own private parts when he is on his own in his bedroom with the door shut (so it is private). He might need help to learn about masturbation (see section 5.2)

4 Encourage positive behaviours

Rewarding appropriate (non-sexual touching) is key to encouraging positive behaviour. It is important to give children feedback on their behaviour so they know what they should be doing. Notice when your child is behaving well and tell them: 'Well done, you behaved very well with that person.'

5.5 My son likes dressing up in women's clothes. What should I do?

Like the rest of the population, sometimes people with intellectual disabilities talk about wanting to 'change' the person they are, and this can include their gender. This can lead them to want to dress in the clothes of the opposite sex or take on the gender role of the opposite sex. There are multiple reasons for this and it is beyond the scope of this book to explore them. Suffice to say that while cross-dressing might only interest a small percentage of the population, it is best understood as just part of the spectrum of human identity and sexuality and not the result of some kind of underlying disorder or 'mental illness'.

DEFINITIONS

Cross-dressing is when people choose to wear clothing considered to be appropriate for the opposite sex — males wearing female clothing and females wearing male clothing. It is quite normal for young children to dress up and pretend to be the opposite sex at some point in time. However, as they become older, our culture tends to find this behaviour a social taboo. Cross-dressing is a complex subject with multiple meanings. Many people who cross-dress are heterosexual and many are not interested in gender reassignment (though a minority are). Some people consider cross-dressing to be a hobby that forms part of their identity as other hobbies do. For others it is a private, sexual fetish, or a way of expressing themselves socially.

Young people with intellectual disabilities may explore cross-dressing as part of their identity or sexuality like anyone else interested in it would. However, often parents worry that that the stigma of cross-dressing will be a part of their child's identity that will lead to difficult situations in the community, as they are vulnerable to others' prejudices (from ridicule and bullying to aggression). This sometimes seems even more difficult when young people with intellectual disabilities or a diagnosis of autism are already considered 'vulnerable' as a result of people's perceptions of their intellectual, communication or physical differences.

For a minority of young people, cross-dressing may represent a desire to be, or they may already feel they are, the opposite sex. Children who grow up feeling that they are in the wrong body often feel isolated and alone, which can lead to a lot of unhappiness. Children who feel this way need a lot of understanding and support.[5]

> Ben is 15 and has a diagnoses of autism and intellectual disability. His parents have noticed that he has been taking clothes from his mother's wardrobe. One day, he returned from school and they noticed he had worn women's tights and underwear under his trousers. His parents are finding it difficult to agree on what to do – they worry about him being ridiculed and bullied, but also about him feeling different because of the cross-dressing. They are concerned that he will become more and more isolated.

---

5   www.mermaidsuk.org.uk is really helpful in providing support and has examples of children's stories about their experiences.

What's the issue?

Younger children often dress up and role play being the opposite sex – this is ordinary. But when children do this during adolescence it is harder to understand. In this situation, as parents you can be faced with the dilemma of supporting your child to explore themselves fully and without shame, whilst also wanting to protect them from negative responses from other people.

As with most of the dilemmas in this book, our general advice is to provide children with the skills and support to make their own decisions as much as possible.

What can we do?

1 Talk to your child about their preferences and behaviour

Ask your child if it is something they want to talk about. Let them know that they are not alone, that lots of people are interested in cross-dressing and for different reasons. Your child might want to let you know what their reasons are, but they might not have figured this out themselves yet. If your child feels they want to cross-dress in order to escape from something they are finding difficult – for example, from some abuse that has happened or from an identity as gay or lesbian – you might want to consider whether counselling could be helpful.

2 Emphasise other interests as much as the cross-dressing

Many people who cross-dress emphasise that this is only one part of their identity or one of their hobbies. Considering this as you would any other hobby and including it in person-centred planning might be important for your child.

3 Help them learn to set their own boundaries and limits

Talk to your child about how others may react to their cross-dressing. Let them know that they do not need to be ashamed of cross-dressing. At the same time, because it is usually 'hidden', some people feel confused by it. When people are confused by something, don't understand it or see something as different, they can act in aggressive ways. Some people who cross-dress may be bullied.

Teach your child to consider their own boundaries. Who would they feel safe to tell, and where would they feel safe enough to do it? Do they want to consider meeting other people who enjoy cross-dressing and having an opportunity to ask questions about how they manage their own limits and boundaries?

In cases where young people and young adults are unable to make these kinds of decisions about how to keep themselves safe, their circle of support may need to consider their best interests. We have worked with young people whose circles of support have helped them to cross-dress in private at home, and to start to meet with other people who cross-dress.

4 Provide or allow them to buy clothes rather than take them from others

One of the problems for Ben and his family in the above example is that he is taking the clothes from his mother's wardrobe. Ben may feel that he has no choice, especially if he is not responsible for his own money or buying his own clothes yet. In order to avoid conflict over clothes being taken, it might be possible for Ben and his family to agree that he can have a budget to buy his clothes (online or in a shop) and agree where he can keep them.

5 Sexual identity

A minority of young people who cross-dress will do so because they feel they want to be, or already are, the opposite sex. Young people who feel like this often describe having to repress how they feel and who they feel they are. If you think this is the case for your child, asking for professional and therapeutic help may be necessary.[6]

6 Consider supporting your child to be 'out and proud'

If your child's cross-dressing is an expression of their sexuality, another route to empowerment for young people with intellectual disabilities who cross-dress, as with all minority identities, may be to be 'out and proud'. This has long been a strategy for women, ethnic minorities, and LGBT groups. Finding a sense of acceptance and belonging by meeting with other people who have the same interests and sense of identity can be important.

Developing healthy schools that promote tolerance and acceptance is part of supporting an out and proud culture.[7]

5.6 My child wants to use pornography. What should I do?

Pornography is a complex and controversial topic that raises major moral, cultural, political, social and health questions in our society. While legal in some forms, pornography divides opinion and provokes strong responses from both its supporters and critics. Needless to say, it is beyond the scope of this chapter to go into all these issues; instead, we will focus on the use of pornography in relation to health and wellbeing.

It is worth pointing out, however, that the sensitive content of this chapter will probably raise some difficult questions and feelings for most readers. This is quite natural, but not

---

6   You can find more information at: www.beaumontsociety.org.uk
7   Information about this can be found at: www.schools-out.org.uk/STK/ Student_Tool_Kit.htm

something that should stop us discussing the subject and considering how it might be used safely. The challenge we face is to recognise those uncomfortable thoughts and feelings, while simultaneously addressing the underlying issues relating to the young person's expression of their sexuality.

DEFINITIONS

Pornography is the depiction of erotic behaviour, in the form of pictures or writing, that leads to sexual arousal and excitement. Pornography lies on a continuum for how we represent sex and sexuality in our society. At one end we have pictures of film stars dressed in glamorous clothes in glossy magazines. James Bond in a tuxedo alongside beautiful women in low-cut dresses, for instance. Most people would be okay with these sorts of images and see them as a healthy depiction of human beauty and sexuality. Further along the continuum the images become more explicit and the clothing people are wearing shrinks until it is non-existent. At this point, we have images of naked people, some of which are seen as tasteful, educational and artistic and others being more suggestive, explicit and exploitative. Next come images of people engaging in sex acts, either alone or with people.

The point at which an image (or set of words) becomes pornographic is not precisely defined and, therefore, it will vary from one person to the next. Some people might think a music video with young scantily clad performers is pornographic, and others will feel it's an acceptable expression of human sexuality. The point here is that there are no fully independent measures for defining pornography – instead it is a value judgement we make. This means that your opinion about the extent to which an image is pornographic is as valid as the next person's.

While there is much debate among individuals, organisations, professions and institutions about what constitutes pornography, ultimately the decision about the extent to which an image is pornographic is set by the courts and tries to reflect general public opinion. This is why certain images that are allowed today were illegal a hundred years ago. For the purposes of this chapter, pornography will refer to images of naked people and images of people engaged in sexual acts. How this definition relates to individual pictures is for you to decide.

> Peter is 15 years old and has a diagnosis of autism. He likes to play games on his computer and chat with friends. Over the last six months his parents have been increasingly worried that he is looking at a range of pornographic websites. When they ask him about this, he becomes very angry and shouts at them. They tried controlling his access to these websites by restricting his access to his computer and blocking Internet access to certain key words, but he became physically aggressive and accused them of trying to control him. He uses a computer password so they cannot check what he is looking at, but have managed to block some sites containing certain words. They are still worried about what he is looking at and how it is affecting his behaviour. They wonder if it is making him more aggressive too.

What's the issue?

While using pornography to become sexually aroused, perhaps while masturbating, is generally viewed as acceptable in today's society, pornographic images that show negative or abusive sexual behaviours towards each other are more problematic. The reason for this is that human beings learn how to behave towards each other by observing other people. We call this 'observational learning', and a large part of what we do is shaped by what we see other people doing. If we see people behaving towards other people in sexually harmful ways, this can lead us to behave similarly.

One of the problems with pornography is that typically it does not represent healthy and balanced sexual relationships. A lot of pornography depicts very distorted fantasies about sex that are not helpful examples of how to behave sexually towards other people. This means it is not a good basis for understanding how to have a positive and respectful relationship with another person.

Therefore *we advise against allowing young people to have unrestricted access to pornography.* Unrestricted access would inevitably mean the young person would see examples of negative and/or unrealistic representations of sexual behaviour. If these are the first (or early) examples of sexual behaviour they observe, they can be particularly powerful in shaping their understanding, views and ideas about sex and how they express their sexuality. There are also illegal images of sexual acts with children and animals that can be found on the Internet. Viewing these types of images can again lead to unhealthy ideas about sexual behaviour and to the possibility of a police investigation followed by prosecution in the courts.

Restricting access to pornographic material would mean either allowing no access to it or vetting and selecting the materials (e.g. DVDs or magazines) that the young person could see.

The Internet

The Internet provides such easy access to the whole range of pornographic images that it needs to be carefully controlled. All mainstream Internet providers have settings for restricting and blocking access to certain sites and key words. This allows you to block access to nearly all pornography involving images of sexual intercourse. It is not possible to block images of naked people, as the human body is not primarily seen as sexual, but Internet access settings will enable you to restrict sites showing actual sexual activity.

If the young person is legally an adult (18 years old) and has the mental capacity to decide for themselves what sort of pornography they see, then under the UK legal system that is their choice. But if they are living in your house and accessing the pornography through your Internet connection, you still have some say over the matter and, again, we would advise controlled access only. If you want further advice about this, contact your local specialist intellectual disability health service team.

What can we do?

The three most common questions families and carers ask in relation to pornography follow below.

1 My child wants to use pornography, what should I do?

If your child is asking to look at pornographic images, depending on your child's age and abilities, it is quite acceptable to say 'no' and not allow them to see pornographic images. For instance, if a pre-pubescent child asked to see some pornographic pictures, this is not appropriate. If they have started puberty and are beginning to explore their sexuality, this is a good opportunity to begin a sex education programme as set out in Chapter 9.

While parents and carers often feel uncomfortable in relation to their children's sexual behaviour, the more important issue is their healthy development and safety. With this in mind, if your child has started puberty and they have the mental capacity to make informed decisions about pornography, you can provide them with pornographic images and materials. This way you can vet and control your child's early experiences of sexual behaviour and help them learn about and develop their sexuality in healthy ways.

2 I think my child is looking at pornography on the Internet. What can I do?

Our advice is not to allow your child to view pornography on the Internet. For the reasons outlined above, there are just too many negative, unhealthy and illegal pornographic images on the Internet, and allowing your child unrestricted access places them at risk.

A first step is to set up 'parental control' restrictions with your Internet service provider (ISP) to block access to particular websites and block searches for key words. All mainstream ISPs provide this service and if your current one doesn't, or you think it is ineffective, move to an ISP with a more robust system for restricting Internet access. Alternatively, there are software packages you can purchase or you can seek specialist advice.

Restricting access to the Internet is technically quite straightforward, but it is not usually the main issue families face. Rather, it is managing the social consequences of placing restrictions on children's access that is often more problematic. Some children respond angrily, even aggressively, when their access to the Internet is restricted, particularly to pornography (even when they don't say it is for this reason).

Our advice is to set up your Internet service restrictions as early as possible, long before it is a potential issue with your child. That way they always know their access is restricted and they are more likely to accept it. If, however, they don't accept it or you are imposing restrictions after you have become aware it is a problem, our advice is to hold firm and maintain the restrictions. Even if you child becomes upset, angry and/or aggressive, keep your Internet access restrictions in place. For a start, it is just too risky to allow them unrestricted access and, in addition (but just as importantly), it is not helpful for you to change your decision when your child behaves in angry or aggressive ways. This just gives them the message that they can control what you do by behaving in these ways and encourages this behaviour the next time.

If your child's behaviour is highly aggressive or extreme in another way, seek immediate advice and support from your local specialist health service.

3 My child is being overly sexual with people/ trying to masturbate in public places. Would this stop or reduce if they used pornography?

Sometimes children and young people behave in ways that indicate they are sexually aroused. For instance, they can rub their genitals against things or with their hands. Or they can be very sexual towards other people, perhaps touching them inappropriately or constantly talking about bodies and sex.

When this happens, parents and carers can conclude that their child is sexually frustrated and wonder if this would reduce if they had access to pornography.

Our advice in this situation is to begin a general sex education and development programme (see Chapter 9) and not to turn to pornography. Problematic displays of sexualised behaviour represent gaps in a child's social skills. Becoming sexually aroused is quite natural and is something we all experience from time to time. Teenage boys, for instance, commonly experience regular erections throughout the day and night. The issue is not the sexual arousal, but rather how we express this. If it is not the right place (e.g. public), we need to learn to control our behaviour in socially appropriate ways.

Essential for learning society's rules is feedback from other people about what is and isn't socially acceptable. This doesn't mean we should be critical of them or their behaviour, rather we just need to consistently point out what they should do instead. For example, if a child begins to masturbate while sitting on the sofa, you might say: 'Oh Peter, masturbating in public is not allowed. If you want to continue, please go to your bedroom.'

Even if your child does not fully understand complex spoken language or spoken language at all, you can still provide them with feedback about how to behave in public. For example, you might simplify what you say: 'No, Peter. No masturbating here. Go to your bedroom.', You can then encourage them to go to their bedroom. Even children and young people with complex and severe intellectual disabilities can still learn appropriate social rules, and this includes how to behave sexually in public.

Pornography addiction

There can be occasions when people become very fixated on pornography and want to use it regularly. If the level of their interest in pornography causes them psychological distress or interferes with their daily lifestyle, it can be seen as a type of *addiction*. If this is the case with your child/young person, then it is best to seek specialist advice and support.

Pornography information sheet for young people

Pornography is sometimes called 'porn' for short. Porn is pictures and films of naked people and sex. The people in the films are having sex, but they are actors. It is okay to use pornography; lots of adults do.

Porn is not like real sex. The actors in porn films are paid to have sex so they sometimes do things that they wouldn't do in real life. In real life, people's bodies are usually different. In real life, women usually have some pubic hair. Men's penises and women's breasts are usually smaller in real life.

Sex in real life usually happens between two people who care about each other's feelings during sex and respect each other.

There are some rules about watching porn that everyone needs to remember. It is important to watch porn in private. This means in a bedroom with the door shut. Remember to make sure that other people cannot hear it, and to turn it off if you leave your bedroom.

There are certain types of porn that are legal and some types that are illegal. It is okay to watch porn that involves adults. It is not okay to watch porn that involves young people or animals. The police can monitor what you watch and which websites you go on even if you delete your history.

It is sometimes difficult to work out what is okay and not okay to look at on the Internet. Once you have seen something, it is not possible to 'unsee' it. Sometimes it is safer to buy DVDs or porn or magazines or watch it on TV, as it is easier to make sure it is legal. Sometimes you have to pay extra to watch porn channels on the TV and so you must have permission to do this from the person that pays the bills.

Some people do not like talking about pornography as it makes them feel embarrassed. It is important to think of other things to talk about with friends and family, like other hobbies or interests.

If you want to learn more about this topic go to:
www.thinkuknow.co.uk

5.7 My son thinks everyone on the Internet is his best friend. How do I keep him safe?

The Internet is a fantastic invention and resource that enables us to learn new things and meet new people, but it also has a darker side. The anonymity of the Internet allows people to pretend to be someone they are not and sometimes commit crimes. For example, everyone who has an Internet account will have had scam email from someone pretending to offer some kind of amazing deal. Or it might even look like an official email from your bank or HMRC. Invariably these emails are scams from people trying to get access to your bank account or computer. Sometimes people's motives are sexual. They ask for naked pictures or engage in sexually explicit chat. Protecting children and vulnerable adults from these types of abuse is very important.

DEFINITIONS

Online safety is about ensuring that children and vulnerable people are protected from harmful experiences they might have via the Internet. Online safety isn't limited to home computers and laptops, but includes mobile phones which can also access the Internet. Being safe online is important and protects people from a variety of potential problem issues, such as harassment, threats, financial fraud, identity theft, bullying, inappropriate sexualised behaviour or any form of exploitation.

Children and young people with intellectual disabilities can do a lot of different things on the Internet that might expose them to risky situations. For example, they can:

- watch inappropriate content and videos, like pornography

- meet people on social networking sites, like Facebook and Twitter

- join online forums and messaging boards

- chat with other people via email, multiplayer games or webcams.

What's the issue?

The issue is how to strike a balance between the benefits of going online and the potential risks associated with it. For example, going onto the Internet can expose your child to any or all of the following problem areas:

- cyber-bullying

- financial fraud and identity theft

- grooming

- adult pornography

- hate crimes

- online gambling

- exposure to inappropriate content

- potential abuse by online predators.

Each and every one of the above problems presents a risk to young people and children. And due to their more limited understanding, children and people with intellectual disabilities are particularly vulnerable to being taken advantage of over the Internet.

Liz is 15 years old and has a mild intellectual disability. She is studying for some GCSEs at school and uses the Internet to help with her course work. She also likes to chat with friends on social media forums. She started puberty three years ago and has shown an interest in having a relationship with boys. She has had sex and relationship lessons at school and her parents have also discussed the topic with her. They have also explained the risks associated with the Internet and have an agreement about how she can use it. Recently she has been spending a lot of time on the Internet, particularly in her bedroom at night. When her parents ask her about this, she says she is chatting with friends. Her parents aren't sure and when they check with her friends' parents, they say their children are not allowed on the computer that late at night. You wonder what is going on and what you can do next.

What can we do?

One option is to stop your child from using the Internet. This will protect them from any inappropriate content or the risk of meeting risky people, but it will also stop them enjoying the benefits of the Internet.

If you don't want to ban Internet use completely, the only other option is to teach your child effective online safety skills and supervise their usage closely. Here are some tips for keeping your child safe online.

1 Discuss the issue with your child and set limits

Discuss the issues of Internet use and explain that they can only access it if they use it responsibly. Explain some of the dangers that come with Internet use and what they need to look out for:

- Place the computer in a family room with the screen facing outwards so you can see what is going on.

- Explain that it is never acceptable to use abusive, bullying or threatening language.

- Ask your child to report any abusive, bullying or threatening language to you.

- Ask your child not to download any unknown files without first checking with you.

- Tell them to take regular breaks from computer use. Ideally, they should take a break at least every 30 minutes.

- Limit the times your child can use the Internet/ computer.

2 Set parental controls

Computers and mobile phones have parental controls that you can set to restrict the websites and content your child can get access to. You can use them to block selected websites, email addresses or searching for certain words, and limit the amount of time the computer is used.

3 If there is a problem, contact your ISP

If your child experiences any inappropriate content online or if they are bullied or abused in any way, contact your ISP. If you are worried about illegal materials or suspicious online behaviour, contact the Child Exploitation and Online Protection centre (CEOP).

5.8 My son is sexually interested in feet/ nappies/phones, etc. What should I do?

Having a sexual interest in body parts (like feet) or things (like phones or nappies) is more common than you might think. The reason for this is that people can become sexually interested in almost anything, depending on the experiences they have in life. Clearly, some fetishes are unhealthy, abusive and even dangerous, but it is worth remembering these are relatively rare and most are simply part of the range of sexual diversity that exists in human lives.

DEFINITIONS

A sexual interest in objects or non-sexual parts of the body is called sexual or erotic fetishism. Generally, sexual fetishism is seen as part of the natural spectrum of sexual activity humans engage in and not as the sign of a mental disorder or pathology. Because human beings tend to keep their sexual activity private, most people are unaware of other people's sexual interests and behaviours. However, anonymous surveys reveal there is much greater diversity in people's sexual behaviour than is commonly represented in mainstream media and culture.

Sexual fetishism only becomes an issue when it becomes public or when it begins to interfere with a person's ordinary life. For example, it might be embarrassing for other family members, or a carer might be concerned that the young person's inability to be discreet about their preoccupations makes them socially vulnerable to bullying or sexual abuse.

The most common sexual fetish we encounter is related to adolescent males being interested in nappies or continence pads. Their interest can vary from just wanting to hold them to wearing them while they masturbate. It is not always clear why this sexual interest arises, but it is usually the case that the adolescent was still wearing nappies when he entered puberty. This association of events can link sexual experiences and nappies together, such that when the young person thinks of sex, he also thinks of nappies. Having an interest in nappies can be problematic for a number of reasons. For instance, the young person may not discriminate between clean and used nappies. Then he might wear the soiled nappy or use it to masturbate with. Or, because young children wear nappies, other people might mistakenly think he is sexually interested in children and accuse him of paedophilia. Or, he might steal them from people's houses or shops. In our experience all these things can and do happen.

> Dan is 16 and enjoys talking about continence pads, buying pads and wearing them. He becomes sexually aroused when touching or using pads. He deliberately urinates in them and hides them. Dan's carers are concerned that if he becomes sexually aroused when looking at continence pads in the supermarket, this will cause alarm to members of the public and he may be mislabelled as 'deviant'. It is possible that his sexual fetish started as a sensory

interest in continence pads, and became associated with sexual feelings as he has gone through puberty. Dan might not understand the social consequences of his preoccupation.

What's the issue?

While fetishes are part of the range of human sexuality, they can present a problem for young people with intellectual impairments. Their more limited social awareness and understanding will mean they are less able to be discreet about their interest or to understand the social implications of talking about or acting on these interests.

Sexual fetishism can cause anxiety in family, friends and carers. It is natural to wonder whether the child's preoccupation represents a deep psychological issue or a quirk that needs to be adapted to. As we stated in Chapter 1, when considering more unusual sexual behaviour it is always important to consider the possibility of sexual abuse – either historic or current. However, for most young people, their preoccupation is likely to be an ordinary part of their sexuality.

What can we do?

1 Understand what their interest is

If you think your child is developing, or has developed, a sexual fetish, it is important to find out as much as possible about it. Of course you will need to be respectful of their privacy and their right to develop their own sexual interests, but we also advise trying to understand as much as you can about their interest, where it might have come from and how they engage with it. This is important in order to check if there are any risks associated with their sexual interest that they might need help managing or avoiding.

2 Let your child know that this is okay and they are not alone

Once you understand why your child is expressing a sexual fetish, you will be in a better place to be able to support them. When you know they are safe, you can give them the message that their sexual interest is okay and nothing to worry about. It just needs to be expressed in the right way.

3 Teach them why privacy is important

Sexual behaviour is largely a private matter in Western societies. If your child is displaying sexualised behaviour in public, this can lead to difficulties and embarrassment. To help them with this, they would benefit from learning the difference between public and private places and parts of the body. 'Public' means somewhere where there is more than one person. 'Private' means a place where someone is on their own and cannot be seen. Private parts of the body are the parts covered by underwear.

To return to the above example, Dan could be reminded that he can look at and use continence pads in his bedroom with the door shut. He may need help to know how to dispose of the pads discreetly and hygienically.

The pack 'Puberty and Sexuality' (Leeds Nursing 2009) includes pictures of public and private places and parts of the body, which is helpful in teaching children about these concepts.

4 Allow access to objects/images in a safe and contained way

In our experience, young people who are denied access to the objects they are preoccupied with tend to gain access to them through inappropriate means, such as stealing. It may be helpful for Dan's parents to let him have access to a limited number of continence pads that are kept in a private drawer.

5 Make the rules explicit

Once your child understands the difference between public and private, they can be taught clear and explicit rules about how to behave in these settings. Dan's carers, for example, may need to write the rules down or use symbols to reinforce the key messages about where/when he can access continence pads and the rules about not involving other people in his interest. As Dan becomes older, it may be that he has the capacity (in terms of the Mental Capacity Act 2005) to make a decision about sharing his interest and sexuality with other consenting adults. In the meantime, he may need the rule to be simplified – that is, he should not show others or ask others to be involved in his sexual interest.

6 Reward behaviours that are appropriate

When your child is behaving appropriately, give them positive feedback on the behaviour. This might sound obvious, but it is often overlooked. Rather than waiting to 'catch them behaving badly', the idea is to 'catch them behaving well'. After all, if we don't provide encouragement and support for positive behaviour, we shouldn't be surprised when it doesn't occur.

If Dan is able to follow the social rules around his preoccupation, it would be helpful to positively reinforce this through social praise or rewards that are motivating to him. Dan would benefit from knowing that his carers are pleased he stuck to the rules because this helps to keep him happy and safe. The rewards need to be frequent enough to make a change – if the interest is intense and happening every day, Dan may need to be reminded of the rules and rewarded for sticking to them twice a day.

7 Seek further support if required

Sometimes sexual fetishes are understandably difficult areas for family carers to address. We would encourage you to seek further support via your GP or school special educational needs coordinator if you feel it is something that you or your child would benefit from help with.

5.9 Sexting, nude selfies and social media: How do I keep my child safe?

Children and young people with intellectual disabilities may be particularly vulnerable. They may find it more difficult to resist peer pressure or to understand the multiple layers of social meaning online. They may have difficulties understanding that people do not always mean what they say (e.g. that someone may say that something nice will happen if you send an image, when it may not).

DEFINITIONS

Sexting is the sharing of sexually explicit images, also known as 'nude selfies', or messages online or through social media. It is increasingly common amongst young people, who tend to see it as part of ordinary life. The danger is that once an image or message has been sent, the young person has no control over where it is saved or shared, and it can be extremely difficult to remove. It is also illegal to share indecent images of children under 18, even if it is you in the picture. It can leave young people vulnerable to bullying, blackmail, unwanted attention and feelings of shame or embarrassment.

What's the issue?

Social media such as Facebook can be both a positive opportunity for children with intellectual disabilities, and a social and emotional minefield! For children who find socialising anxiety-provoking, the opportunity to connect with others online, and not to have to worry about interpreting body language or how they are coming across, is a relief. For others, the rules around privacy and online social etiquette can be difficult to comprehend.

> Davinder is 14 and has been using his mobile phone to text people and to use Facebook. His carer recently checked his Facebook profile and noticed that he had asked out another boy on the public profile. Underneath this were homophobic comments from other children, which Davinder had not deleted – he did not seem to be aware that they were abusive. His carer asked Davinder if she could look at his private messages and she found that somebody had asked him to send a nude selfie.

Davinder, like most children, is keen to develop friendships and intimate relationships. Doing this online probably feels easier than doing it in real life. Davinder may have found it difficult to express his sexuality at school, but easier to do this online.

 What can we do?

1 Consider setting up social network protection software

There are various free software programs available to parents that enable them to monitor their children's activities on social media. These programs offer options such as receiving email alerts when your child's activities make references to certain words (such as sex, drugs, suicide), or when your child becomes friends with someone of a different age to them. They can provide filtering options, so that your child cannot access certain sites, and time limits, to limit your child's access to social media.

2 Talk about their online life and teach children how to use social media

Monitoring software cannot keep children 100 per cent safe. Children need to know that it is okay to talk to an adult if they are upset about something or if they have done something they regret, such as sending a nude selfie. Sometimes parents and carers worry about whether their child is emotionally ready to learn about these issues. Our advice is that if, like Davinder, they are using mobile phones and social media, they need to know the dangers and how to keep themselves safe.

Children also need opportunities to learn the skills they need to keep themselves safe online. Davinder may benefit from his carer teaching him how to use the privacy settings on Facebook. She may want to teach him the differences between private posts and public posts. Davinder may need to know about the difference between conversations between friends (which can be public), and conversations between people who fancy each other and/or want to be in an intimate relationship (which should be private). He would benefit from knowing that not everyone is who they say they are online.

Davinder may benefit from learning about bullying and how it is different to 'banter'. This includes homophobic bullying. If Davinder is being called names or people are saying things to him repeatedly that make him feel uncomfortable, upset or embarrassed, and he has tried to tell them to stop, this is bullying. Homophobic bullying – when someone feels bullied because of their actual or perceived sexuality – is not okay. Davinder should know that it is okay to express his sexuality and to ask out other boys. At the same time, he might need to think about how to handle bullying online as well as in real life.

3 Teach children about sexting

Davinder would benefit from knowing what sexting is, what a nude selfie is and what the dangers are in sending messages or images online. Davinder's carer will need to talk to him about trust and how people can change their mind, or not do as they say they will, especially when a relationship breaks up. This means that even if someone promises they won't share your image or message, they might change their mind and send it later on. This could make Davinder feel upset and embarrassed. Reinforcing these messages via a social story may help Davinder to process it and remember the information.

4 Teach children about the stepping stones to relationships

In our experience, young people often need support to understand the stepping stones to developing a romantic or intimate relationship, and the unwritten rules around this. Many young people jump straight to asking people out or asking people for sex. To help young people understand, there is a useful resource from the Family Planning Association (FPA) that includes a cartoon story about the steps to building a relationship with someone.

5 Ensure children have opportunities to develop friendships and relationships in real life

When children lack opportunities to develop real-life relationships, they may retreat to an online world. If children need support to develop friendship skills and make social connections, we would recommend the resources at the end of the chapter.

5.10 What issues might my child have around body image and physical differences?

Body image is the mental picture someone has of their body and how they feel about that picture. It is shaped by other people's reactions to us, our feelings about our bodies and whether our bodies are seen as a 'problem'. Whether we have control over decisions about our bodies and what happens to them is also important in shaping body image.

When children have physical differences associated with disabilities or genetic conditions such as cerebral palsy, often their bodies can cause other people to judge them and be curious. They may stare or ask questions about the person's body ('what happened to you?'), which they wouldn't think of asking people without disabilities. Sometimes children with physical differences and their parents/carers can feel vulnerable in social situations. They might feel unsure of how people will respond or what they will ask (Rice *et al.* 2003). It can take time to find a way to feel in control of these interactions and this isn't always an easy journey for parents/carers. At the same time, the process of adapting to difference can be one that leads to an improved understanding of what really matters to you, and what it means to be human.

Positive images of physical differences are still fairly rare, but gradually increasing. The much-loved children's programme CBeebie's 'Mr Tumble' includes children with disabilities in every episode; toy companies are starting to develop toys representing children with disabilities (e.g. the Toys Like Us campaign – Playmobil); and we are beginning to see the inclusion of children with disabilities in storybooks, not just as 'special' guests but as an ordinary part of the story, like in Quentin Blake's *The Five of Us*.

> Madison is 8 years old and was born with a physical disability – she has limited function in her left hand and hemiplegia. Her parents have noticed that other people tend to stare at her when she has her frame, though she doesn't seem bothered by this. Her father is keen for her to be able to walk without it as he feels that she will always be stigmatised by it. Her mother worries about how to support her through her teenage years – she herself found adolescence a difficult time when she compared herself to others and felt self-conscious, so what will this be like for her daughter?

What's the issue?

Madison's parents are struggling with wanting to protect their daughter from the stigma of a physical disability. They are struggling with their own thoughts and feelings about her physical difference and anticipating that she might find the comparison between her body and 'non-disabled' bodies hard. Her father is picking a common strategy of minimising difference as a way of supporting his daughter. That is understandable and lots of young people and adults with disabilities tell us that there are times when this is a useful strategy. However, there are times when minimisation of difference doesn't work and families may need a wider range of ways to cope with their concerns about difference. At this stage, Madison doesn't seem to have the same difficult thoughts and feelings about her disability as her parents.

What can we do?

1 Love and respect your own body in order to teach your child she can love and respect hers

Madison's parents might take some time to examine their own body image. In order to teach her to love and accept the body parts that others might see as a 'problem', they need to accept and love the parts of their bodies that they don't like. This might not be an easy task – changing our view of ourselves is tough (this is even more of a reason to support children to have a healthy and positive view of themselves from the beginning). For Madison's parents, changing their body image may involve acknowledging their own running commentary in their minds (I'm fat, I'm ugly) and taking some steps to change this. These steps might include:

- 'Radical acceptance': Radical acceptance is not the same as 'giving up'. It means truly accepting something in your heart and soul and not fighting it. In this case, the acceptance may be in relation to your own body and the parts that you see as being less than perfect. It means accepting your body as it is *and* seeing it as beautiful.

  Radical acceptance in relation to disability can be a challenging idea. Many parents will still feel in the 'searching' phase (Miller 1994) in relation to their child – searching for therapeutic interventions/surgery, etc. that may improve physical functioning. Only you will know when you have done enough and when moving on to accepting what you can't change will be the best option for your child.

- Focusing on the quality or value you want people to notice when you first meet them, rather than focusing on the part of your body you don't want people to notice: For example, do you want people to notice your warmth/ friendliness/compassion? Can this be more important than appearance?

- Thinking about the messages from the media you might have internalised: We live in a society where we are constantly bombarded with messages about needing to fix our hair/skin/wrinkles/size…but companies need to create these insecurities in order to grab our attention and persuade us to buy their products. Recognising when we are being influenced by these messages can be a step towards realising that we do have the capacity to define for ourselves what is beautiful or acceptable in terms of appearance.

Madison's parents might feel that they aren't in a position to worry about their bodies as it isn't 'as bad' as being a wheelchair user or needing a walking aid – yet we have all been in a position of having our bodies compared to others. If this has happened to you, how did being compared to others make you feel? How did you respond and how could your response give a positive message to your child about how to cope with being compared?

2 Think about how you model to your children how to respond to other people's questions/looks

Madison's parents might need to prepare themselves for other people's reactions and think about how they want to respond to these – this is crucial because it will model to their daughter how she should feel about her body and how she can cope with social interactions.

Responses might include inviting yourself into others' conversations – letting them know that Madison is a girl who enjoys having fun just like any other child, and anyway, we all look different from each other. It might include smiling and walking away, or educating the person about Madison's disability – what she can do independently/with support. It might involve letting them know that Madison's physical disabilities are not a 'tragedy' or something to pity, but a part of her identity just as her brown hair is. It might include teaching other children that everyone is different from each other – our skin, hair and eye colour, and whether we need a wheelchair or not. How we treat each other is more important than how we look.

3 *The Emperor's New Clothes* – who you are and what you do is more important

The Emperor's New Clothes is a children's story that contains a metaphor to explain that what is beautiful or what we think will make us feel good is often an illusion – what we think of as perfect is usually created, we can be duped into believing that things should be a certain way and that, if they are, we will be loved and admired. It is usually with age and wisdom that we begin to realise that what we think will make us happy may not be what actually makes us happy. What matters to you and what messages do you want to give your child?

Make sure that your child's body is represented in media and toys that you give them. Madison's parents may want to think about her toys, television programmes and stories – do they include positive images of children with physical disabilities?

4 Teach children coping skills directly

Sometimes children need a bit more direct help to see themselves as a whole person and not just a reflection of their body and how similar it is to others' bodies. They might also need a bit of help to practise responding to other people's comments in a way they feel comfortable with (try to think about their personality when you do this and not expect a quiet child to be confrontational or dramatic, for example). You could create a scrapbook or collage with your child to address these kinds of questions:

- What do I like about my inside and outside?

- What are my qualities: personality, physical characteristics (body), passions, interests, style (clothes/fashion sense)?

- What are the things I can do to feel better about my body and myself?

- What are the things I can do to deal with hurtful situations?

- What is one thing I can do to take care of myself when something happens that is hurtful?

Resources
Friendship

Blake, Q. (2014). *The Five of Us*. London: Tate Publishing.

Frankel, F. (2010) *Friends Forever: How Parents Can Help Their Kids Make and Keep Good Friends*. San Francisco, CA: John Wiley & Sons.

Madorsky Elman, N. and Kennedy-Moore, E. (2003) *The Unwritten Rules of Friendship: Simple Strategies to Help Your Child Make Friends*. London: Little, Brown and Company.

www.thinkuknow.co.uk

Relationships

FPA Talking together… about sex and relationships. Available at www.fpa.
  org.uk/product/talking-together-about-sex-and-relationships, accessed
  9 April 2016.

Puberty and sexuality

www.bbc.co.uk/learningzone/clips/touching-yourself-in-private-
  female/10833.html

Body image

http://bodygossip.org

www.bodyimagemovement.com

Chapter 6

FEELINGS

This chapter looks at the emotional issues for both children and their carers that can arise during puberty.

6.1 I'm worried my child is vulnerable to abuse. What can I do?

The possibility of sexual exploitation or abuse of children with intellectual disabilities is a fear that can underlie the daily experience of parents/carers. This anxiety reflects a real fact about young people with disabilities – they are more vulnerable than many of their non-disabled peers. They might not understand what is happening around them, or be able to communicate when something bad has happened. Or they might engage in risky behaviours, like engaging in a public sexual act, which could see them taken advantage of. These, and many other factors, mean that young people with intellectual disabilities are more vulnerable. But this doesn't mean they need be at any greater risk.

DEFINITIONS

Sexual abuse occurs when one person takes advantage of another person for their own sexual gratification. Sexual abuse involves any kind of unwanted sexual contact, from groping or kissing to penetrative sex. Sexual abuse is illegal and when it is discovered it is investigated by the police, and when there is enough evidence prosecutions will be sought. All sexual contact between people must be consensual to be legal, and at the point where one person wants it to stop, it becomes illegal to continue. Sex with children under the age of 16 years or with people who do not have the mental capacity to consent to sex is also illegal.

What's the issue?

Young people with intellectual or physical disabilities may be more vulnerable to sexual abuse for multiple reasons. They are sometimes treated as 'asexual' or as 'emotionally naïve' and miss out on SRE or information that could help protect them. They may not have the verbal communication skills to be able to tell someone about an abusive experience and, even if they do, they may not be aware that they have a right to complain, or may not be listened to. And they are more likely to rely on adults for support with intimate and personal care, which creates increased opportunities for abuse, especially if there are a number of different carers in different environments.

One way of managing this might be to 'hold on' to children in order to keep them safe. However, we know that overprotection can inadvertently increase risks, as it doesn't give children the chance to learn the skills they need to manage risks themselves. As a first line of protection, children need to learn how to have positive and healthy relationships with other people, and this includes sexual relationships. That is not to say that it is the responsibility of children and young people to ensure they are not sexually exploited; it is the responsibility of all human beings not to hurt or exploit anyone else.

What can we do?

1 Teach your child the names of body parts
All children benefit from this. If something happens that they are uncomfortable with or if they are abused, they need to be

able to tell you what's happened. If they don't know the names of their own body parts, they won't be able to do this.

2 Teach *all* children the underwear rule (NSPCC Pants Campaign)

The NSPCC recommends teaching children that their bodies and the parts of their bodies in their underwear are private; that their bodies belong to them; that they can say 'no' to things that make them uncomfortable and if they feel upset or worried they should speak up about it even if they have been told to keep it a secret.

3 Listen to children and help them make independent decisions

We are in a position to listen to children, take their views seriously and think carefully about areas of their lives of which they can be in charge. As parents you can teach your children to have their own voice and make their own independent decisions, so that children can also begin to have the confidence to communicate 'no' to unwanted touch or sexual contact. Helping children to make independent decisions and choices can sometimes be time consuming. It might start with things like making choices about clothing, food and activities. It is also important to have a plan to support the development of independent living skills. If children can manage to toilet independently, it reduces the opportunity for others to abuse them.

4 Teach older children what kinds of relationships are okay and not okay

Younger children need to know that it is not okay for anyone to look at or touch the parts of the body that are covered by their underwear. It is also not okay for anyone to ask to look at or see their private body parts.

When children require support with intimate and personal care, this is more complicated. In these circumstances it is really important that there is a care plan put in place for children who require this, made in collaboration with the child if possible. Having a consistent and stable support team to do this is likely to minimise risk, compared to just having one person that does it all the time, or lots of different people.

Young people with intellectual disabilities are most often sexually abused by people familiar to them. It is therefore important not to give a message that implies only 'bad' people or strangers are a risk, as realistically this is not the case.

Young people need to know that:

- It is okay to have a romantic relationship and/or sex with someone who is over 16, if both are able to choose whether they have sex, both agree, and both make a decision about using condoms or contraception.

- It is not okay to have a romantic relationship and/or sex with a member of staff. This includes staff at school, personal assistants, care staff. And it is not okay to have a romantic relationship and/or sex with a member of your family.

5 Teach the young person to identify abuse and to tell someone

Your child might be able to understand 'dangerous' situations and learn some personal safety skills. The Green Flag Red Flag personal safety programme asks children to identify 'green flag' and 'red flag' situations in relation to inappropriate behaviour, bribes and threats. Kimberly King's book *I Said No* (2008) is an example of this. It teaches children that their private parts are private and so there are usually only a few people who should be allowed to see them, including parents and the GP. It teaches children that green flag situations make children feel happy and good. Green flag people include parents. Red flag situations make them feel confused, sad or angry. This might include someone offering them money or other treats to show them their private parts, or telling them that they will get in trouble unless they let them look at their private parts (or the other way around). If they identify a red flag situation they need to try to (1) say 'no', (2) get away, (3) tell a helper.

6 Support if it has happened

If a child or young person with an intellectual disability experiences sexual abuse, they should be supported with this immediately. After the event they are likely to feel a range of emotions. Some might be bad and frightening, but some might also be positive, such as feeling desired. This can be confusing and, unless it is addressed, it could place them at risk of future abuse. This might require specialist support and you can ask for help from your GP or advice from charities such as Respond[1] or the NSPCC.[2]

6.2 How do I help my child express their feelings?

Feelings are important. The feelings we have throughout the day reflect our general wellbeing and what has been happening in our life. When life is generally going well, we feel positive and happy; and when something is wrong we have more negative and troublesome feelings. As a rule, we want people we care about to be happy and to share this experience with them. And when they feel sad or unhappy, we want them to be able to express this so we can understand what is wrong and then maybe do something about it. This is important because when people can't effectively express how they feel, they will often express it through their physical actions, and this can be quite challenging. Expressing how we feel is often called 'emotional literacy'.

---

1   www.respond.org.uk
2   www.nspcc.org.uk

DEFINITIONS

What are feelings and emotions? Emotions are sensations that we feel in our bodies, depending on what has happened to us. This is a really important point because it means that we cannot change how we feel at any given point in time any more than we can change what has happened to us. Our feelings are our past showing up in the present and until we invent a time machine, we simply cannot change them. Unfortunately, our culture often gives us the opposite message and encourages us to think we can change and control how we feel. Statements like 'Don't worry, be happy' or 'Stop crying' are commonplace, but the truth is we can no more choose to stop feeling sad than we can just choose to be happy. If we want to feel something different, we need to do new things so that we can have a new history.

While it would be wonderful to only experience positive emotions, that is just not possible. When psychologists conduct research into human emotions, they consistently find that we are more likely to feel negative than positive emotions. Why? Because negative emotions let us know when something is wrong and there are simply many more ways for things to be wrong in life than right. Consider the feelings of hunger, thirst or loneliness. Having just the right amount of food, water and social contact will ensure we feel in balance with life and therefore happy. But this moment will not last because every second we are not eating, drinking or with friends, we are gradually becoming hungrier, thirstier and lonelier. There is quite a narrow range of experience for our bodies to feel 'just right' in comparison to the many levels of hunger, thirst or loneliness. It's a bit like trying to stand a book upright – the laws of physics tell us there are many more ways for it to fall over than to stand vertically.

Emotions are a barometer for what has been happening in our lives. When things are going well, we are content and happy, whereas our negative emotions let us know that something is wrong and that something has to change to put it right. Finally, it is important to stress that you do not need to be able to speak in order to express your emotions. Signing or picture cards can work just as well – see Jack's story on page 133.

What's the issue?

To be able to express how we are feeling, we first have to notice the physical sensation in our body and then we have to label it accurately. In other words, we need to be aware of the bodily sensations associated with feeling tired, bored or hungry, and then use the right words to describe this experience. If we are tired, but we say we are hungry, then people around us are more likely to give us food than to help us to bed. Likewise if we are feeling anxious or angry because something has (or hasn't) happened, then we need to label experience correctly before people around us know something is wrong.

So how do we help people talk accurately about the world inside their skin? We only know what something is called when someone tells us its name. However, teaching people to talk about their emotions is difficult because the person doing the teaching cannot 'see' another person's inner experience. It is a bit like trying to teach a child the colours of the rainbow over the telephone. You can't see what the child is pointing to when they say 'red' or 'blue', so you don't know when to give praise for correct answers.

Although we can't 'see' another person's emotional state directly, we can have a guess about what they are likely to be feeling. We can do this by observing their behaviour and/or by knowing things about their life circumstances. For instance, if we know when a child last ate, we can have a good guess at when they are likely to be hungry. Similarly, if we see a child eating quickly, we can assume they are hungry and might say: Oh you're hungry.' This is how we teach people to label what they are experiencing inside their body. In short, this is how we teach them to express their feelings.

But there is another, more important, element to be aware of when we teach people to talk about their inner world of emotions. When we label a person's emotional experience in a particular way, we also model for them how to behave towards that emotion. Consider a situation when a parent walks into the bathroom and sees a spider on the floor. If they yell, 'It's a spider!', throw their arms in the air and run out of the room, the child learns two things: first, that the thing on the floor is called a 'spider', and second that the way to behave towards it is to run away. We learn what something is called *and* how to behave towards it.

The same principle for learning about how to behave towards events inside our body applies to events outside our body. If a person labels another person's emotional experience in a calm and contained way, the message is 'I know what you are feeling and it's okay'. Even if the emotional state is not very nice, like anger or boredom, the message is that it's okay to have these experiences and they are not something to be overwhelmed by. Conversely, if the person gets angry, shouts or kicks the dog when the child feels upset, they also model how to behave towards this feeling. The message the child receives is: 'This is how to respond to what you are feeling.' Providing a calm response to a child's difficult emotional experience is called 'emotional containment' and is key to helping us become emotionally literate and mature people.

Sarah is 13 years old and has an autistic spectrum diagnosis and severe intellectual disabilities. She lives with her parents and older brother. Sarah has limited speech and often uses signs to communicate to let people know what she is doing and what she wants. But there are also times when Sarah becomes upset and tearful and her family and teachers do not know why. They wonder if it might be related to being anxious or scared about something. When Sarah is in this mood she can become oppositional and sometimes aggressive if she is asked to do something. Usually she is left alone at these times and she usually calms down. But this is not always possible (e.g. at transition times like the end of the school day when she has to get on the bus to go home) and this can lead to incidents of challenging behaviour. And at the same time, people want to understand what Sarah is feeling and why, so they can be more sensitive to her needs and maybe do something about it. People are very frustrated at not knowing how Sarah feels.

 What can we do?

The first step is to help children and young people to label accurately what they are feeling. Once this has been established, the next step is to help them to learn to say *why* they are feeling what they are feeling. For example, when you tell someone you are feeling happy or sad, you will usually also tell them what has happened to leave you feeling this way.

We can teach children to label their internal world by telling when they are likely to be feeling different things. For instance, we can say, 'Oh, Johnnie, you are feeling tired/hungry/bored/angry', depending on what we think Johnnie is feeling based on what we know has happened to him or how he is behaving at this moment in time. The more systematic and consistent we are with our labels, the easier it will be to learn them. If one person labels an experience 'angry' and another says 'annoyed', it can be hard to know which is the correct label.

Here is a four-step programme for how to teach emotional literacy skills. Please note that you do not have to complete the whole programme for it to be effective. Just doing step 1 will help the child understand what they are feeling, even if they never get onto expressing it directly themselves in steps 2, 3 and 4.

1 Label the emotion

Spot when the child is likely to be feeling any emotion and say: 'Oh, Johnnie, you're feeling angry/tired/hungry, etc.' If the child has limited vocal language, it's often a good idea to supplement what you say with a Makaton sign.

If you are not sure what a child is feeling but he is in some way distressed and you want to provide emotional containment, it's okay to say: 'Johnnie, I'm not sure what you are feeling, but I'll be here with you until you start to feel better'. Try to avoid guessing and, if you are not sure, it's better either to say nothing or that you don't know what the child is feeling as this at least provides emotional containment.

2 Encourage the child to tell you what he is feeling

When you feel the child appreciates that you are labelling his experience (he will often look at you), encourage him to repeat the label back to you – for example, 'Johnnie, you're feeling tired. How are you feeling? [Try to prompt him] T...t...ti... tir...tire...tired'. Then praise him if he makes a sound or says the word.

Do not ask the child what he is feeling before you are 100 per cent confident he knows the answer. Doing so can undermine his morale and it's also a missed learning opportunity. If in doubt, tell the child what he is feeling and then ask him – for example, 'Johnnie, you're feeling tired. How are you feeling?'

3 Tell him why he is feeling what he is feeling

When he is consistently labelling his internal world, he next needs to be able to say why he is feeling it. Again, it can help to tell him this initially so he becomes accurate at reporting the contexts that lead to different emotions.

For example, 'Johnnie, you're feeling angry... How are you feeling? [Verbally prompt] A...An...Ang...that's right, "angry". Well done!... You're feeling angry because you want to go outside." Then prompt him to say or sign this back to you.

4 Encourage the child to tell you why he is feeling what he is feeling

Gradually shape up his ability to explain why he is feeling a particular emotion. We do this by building up sentences that refer to important events around him. Even if it is a single word, it can still be useful.

For example, a child might say or sign 'angry', and when asked why he is angry, he might say/sign 'stop', meaning he wants to stop doing what he is doing.

How long it takes to teach a child effective emotional literacy varies. We have known some children to pick it up in weeks, while others can take months and even years. While emotional literacy training can easily be incorporated into daily routines, it can be hard to maintain consistency for long periods and across settings. That said, once the skill is learned the young person will have it for the rest of their life, making the investment of time and effort worthwhile.

> Jack was 10 years old and had Down's syndrome and a severe learning disability. He could say ten or so key words but otherwise used Makaton and pictures to communicate. He had a few favourite activities, but when he wasn't doing them he would often hit people hard on the head. Eventually he was excluded from school and it looked like he would have to go to residential school. As a last resort his family and school set up an intensive Positive Behaviour Support programme, which amongst other things taught him to express his emotions with Makaton signs. After ten months of daily support, Jack was independently signing when he was happy, sad and bored and it was no coincidence that his aggression levels dropped simultaneously.

6.3 My daughter seems very moody, what can I do?

Most people will remember from their own childhood that the teenage years and moodiness tend to go together. You might also remember that thankfully this stage didn't last forever. This is the same for young people with intellectual disabilities, and you can survive it! There are lots of reasons why mood swings can happen during puberty. Puberty is triggered by the release of hormones, which means that young people often experience fluctuations and surges in hormones at this time. This doesn't mean that there is nothing you can do to help your child. The reason that 'moods' might cause a challenge is that this is likely to be the first time your child has experienced these rapid changes in their feelings and body. They are just beginning to understand what's happening and learning how to handle it. At the same time, there are changes that happen in relationships and family dynamics as young people grow up (these are addressed more in Section 6.4). There are changes in appearance, in self-identity and sexual desire, which also create challenges for young people and can contribute to moodiness.

> Lily is 11 and has a severe intellectual disability. She has been waking up in a 'bad mood' and seems much more frustrated and impatient than usual. Sometimes this leads to behaviours that her mum is finding really challenging, like hitting out at her sisters.

What's the issue?

Most children can find it difficult to express their feelings, needs and wishes in a straightforward way. These skills take time to develop and require a secure relationship with an adult who can help the child make sense of their feelings. Unfortunately, not all children have had this in their early lives. Often children with more severe intellectual disabilities can have extra difficulties with emotional understanding and expression. Lily may be using her behaviour because she doesn't yet have the skills to tolerate her frustration and express it in another way. At the same time, it is not okay for her to hit her sisters.

What can we do?

1 Investigate other possible causes for your child's behaviour

All children are affected by the ordinary ups and downs of life and family life. It is important to remember that there may be many reasons for a child's behaviour and mood. Lily's mum might talk to her daughter and those who support her about what's going well and not so well for her at school and home. Issues like bullying, divorce, house moves or more subtle changes to routines can lead to 'moodiness' and behavioural challenges, which are an expression of distress. We would not want to miss these issues by attributing everything to a child's hormones or puberty.

2 Talk to your child about what's happening to her body and feelings

Lily would benefit from knowing as much information as she can manage about what's happening to her body and why her feelings keep changing. We have provided some advice about how to do this in Section 4.1.

3 Try to adjust the demands of the day, depending on what she can handle

There might be certain situations that Lily would find more difficult to handle on a particular day, and where her frustration and behaviour could lead to conflict. Her mum might decide to have some flexibility in the routine so that Lily can have days where she doesn't have as many demands and she can have some space to herself.

4 Help your child get a good night's sleep and look after her body

Keeping our bodies healthy reduces our vulnerability to 'mood swings'. This might seem straightforward but it is often overlooked. Lily could have some help to learn the skills of keeping healthy: making sure she has a longer sleep, drinks water, eats fruit and vegetables and addresses any aches and pains in her body.

5 Be with your child in her feelings

One of the most important things you can do when your child is distressed is to convey to her the message that you 'get it', that you are with her, and she is worth being there for. You don't have to agree with your child's behaviour, or feel the same thing she feels, but matching the intensity and rhythm of her emotion will help her feel that she isn't alone. This is known as 'attunement' and means matching the emotional intensity of the person you're with. The most powerful way of doing this is non-verbally, which means matching the rhythm, tone and volume of your voice (that doesn't mean you need to shout) to that of your child. This is good news for parents who worry that their child might not understand their verbal communication. It is the *way* you convey the message that matters the most.

When Lily becomes distressed in frustration with her sisters, you might say something to her like: 'You really really wanted them to play it your way! You're so cross about it! It's hard not to have things your way. I'll wait here with you until you start to feel better.'

6 Teach your child some self-soothe skills

Helping your child to manage her feelings by being with her (as in step 5) is the basis for helping children to manage their feelings by themselves. At the same time, children with intellectual disabilities can also benefit from extra teaching about how to manage themselves when they are very stressed. There are some good resources, such as Mosley and Grogan's

The Big Book of Calmers, which are full of ideas. The first author has also had experience of developing self-soothe boxes with children. These are shoeboxes that children decorate and fill with items that help them to feel calm. They might include things that are meaningful to the child (a photo that they connect with or a trinket) and sensory items such as bouncy balls, bubbles, playdoh and handerchiefs fragranced with lavender or other scents.

7 Teach your child that she can control her behaviour even if she can't control her feelings

Chapter 6.2 has advice on how to develop children's emotional literacy skills; that is, their ability to identify and label their feelings. This is usually a really important step in children beginning to manage and communicate their feelings. At the same time, it can be helpful to let children know that they can't help how they feel, but they can make some choices about how to act when they are angry/upset/sad. For example, Lily might need to know it is okay to stamp her feet and shout when she is angry, but it is not okay to hit or hurt herself or other people. In the scenario above, Lily's mum might decide to match her daughter's feelings (as in point 5) and, at the same time, let her know she won't allow her to hit people or do things she'll later feel bad about. If Lily manages not to hit her sisters, her mum might praise her for making a smart choice when she was angry.

8 Plan some good things for yourself

Taking care of yourself is absolutely essential. Our experience is that parents often neglect their own needs and feel by the end of the day that they have no energy left to do anything for themselves. You need to be okay in order for your children to be okay: be kind to yourself, build your own support system and know that your feelings are normal. It is challenging parenting a teenager!

6.4 Teenage emotional states – childhood to adulthood – what can I expect?

Often, adolescence is characterised by a child's dilemma of wanting to stay little and be looked after, while at the same time wanting to be an independent adult. In order to develop this independence, young people are often repelled by parents – in public they disown them and find them embarrassing. Parents have to work hard not to take their teenager's rejection personally. Their children still need them to show concern, to help them feel safe by implementing boundaries and to stop them feeling alone.

DEFINITIONS

Between the ages of 13 and 18 years young people go through a number of emotional and social changes as well as physical ones. It is a period of time when they begin to explore who they are and how they are different from others, including their parents. Their relationships with their peers become more and more important and their connection with their family can loosen. During this period, as they move from childhood into adulthood they can become more concerned with what their friends think than what their parents think or say. And at this same time they begin to want to have romantic and sexual relationship with partners. This is quite natural though it can be a challenge for parents as they see their child moving physically and emotionally into adulthood.

What's the issue?

Adolescence is a time when children start to make choices for themselves and manage risk associated with those choices. Children with intellectual disabilities need opportunities to learn these lessons just like all children do. The same dilemmas occur for children with intellectual disabilities, though it may be harder to manage perhaps more exaggerated swings between seeming little and in need of protection, and wanting independence.

How will they handle risk if they don't have a chance to practise in the safety of the relationships that are most important to them?

> Sadie is 15 years old. She has Down's syndrome. Her parents feel that she sees herself as an adult and she is desperate for independence and time away from them. She wants to go to discos, to have a boyfriend, and to minimise differences between her and her peers. Her parents are concerned that she isn't ready for this yet. They are also aware that there are times when she wants to play with toys or play games on her own that other children would find 'babyish'.

What can we do?

1 Letting go vs holding on – balancing over protection and under protection

First let's recognise that adolescence can be a tricky time for parents as well as children! Children's moods can change quickly, arguments may be frequent and children may become more private, wanting to spend time away from the house and with friends.

Yet children with intellectual disabilities need what all children need – for parents to learn to 'let go' and allow them space for developing new attachments and forming their separate identities. 'Letting go' is more of a mindset – one that conveys to children that they can make choices separately from us as parents, and they can challenge our expectations of them. Letting go is also about parents giving themselves permission to have some things in their lives for themselves, and some space away from the family without feeling overwhelming guilt.

Holding children back won't prepare them for adulthood. Accepting that there are real dangers may be necessary – we can only protect children through helping them to take 'safe' or positive risks, with the confidence that they will turn back to their parents/carers if they need help or support and that support will be offered.

2 Chronological age vs developmental age

Sadie's parents might be struggling with the apparent differences in her developmental needs – on the one hand, she wants to be grown up and act like 'her age' or older; on the other hand, she wants to play with toys for younger children. It might be tempting to think: 'Sadie is 15 but she is really like an 8-year-old so she can't be ready for life experiences that a 15-year-old would be.' While this is completely understandable, in our experience this kind of approach tends to lead to overprotection and difficulties with letting young people grow up. Another approach might be to accept Sadie as she is and to make your support a bit more fluid. Sadie is a young person whose body is growing up and whose sexual feelings are real. She might need help to understand this and to develop her relationships skills. At the same time, she isn't ready to give up the toys and things that make her feel safe and happy – she might need to have space to play, and for this to be okay.

3 Maintaining boundaries

Children will push boundaries – teenagers especially will not follow your boundaries completely but might be close enough. They might tell you that you are being unfair, unreasonable, that they aren't going to listen and why should they?! Keep repeating the boundaries – they do want you to show you care, that they matter. You may need to pick your battles!

6.5 My child wants a girlfriend/ boyfriend, but I'm worried they'll be rejected. How can I help?

When surveys are conducted into what people want most in life, having a job and a partner (i.e. girlfriend, boyfriend or spouse) are usually top of the list. A job means having something to do that is valued and meaningful. It gives us a role and position in society and of course it earns us money so we can buy the things we need. And having a partner enables us to love and feel loved. Being in a loving relationship is something nearly everyone wants in life, and when we are not in a relationship we can feel lonely and lost. Wanting to have a girlfriend or boyfriend is likely to reflect this core human need, and disabled people are no different in this regard.

DEFINITIONS

What is a loving relationship? Loving relationships often include physical intimacy and sexual contact but not always. So while sex is not an absolute requirement for a loving relationship, it normally plays a central role.

Of course, relationships involve much more than sex. Socially, having a partner means we have someone to share our lives with. This can be emotional or practical or both. For instance, a partner will share our joys and successes and help us when we need it. They support us emotionally when times are hard and are there when we need a friend. Practically, they will share life's daily tasks, such as shopping, cleaning the house or holding the other end of a tape measure. Having a partner to share all of life's ups and downs makes life easier, and more fun.

The two main reasons people want to have relationships with each other are biological and social. Biologically, having children is a central reason for people wanting to have relationships and, of course, this will typically involve sexual intercourse. In evolutionary terms we want to have relationships with people we are sexually attracted to in order to reproduce. Being in a relationship means there are two parents supporting the offspring and we see this pattern throughout the animal kingdom. But for human beings, sexual contact is much more than just a route to reproduction. It can also be an expression of important human desires like, love, intimacy, connection and tenderness.

This chapter will look at the issue of how to support romantic relationships between disabled young people and this may or may not include any level of sexual contact.

PLEASE NOTE: In the UK sexual intercourse is illegal for children under the age of 16 years and for young people and adults who lack the capacity to consent to sexual relations. For the purposes of this chapter we will assume that the children and young people we refer to have the capacity for the level of sexual activity they are engaging in. For more information about the law and the legal framework for supporting people with disabilities to have sexual relations, please see Chapter 8.

What's the issue?

Disabled children usually want the same kinds of things as other children and this often includes having a relationship with someone. But the nature of a child's disability can present them with particular and additional barriers that make having a relationship harder to achieve. For example, if they have difficulty communicating, it is difficult for them to express how they feel and what they want from a potential partner. And if they have a physical disability, they may find it harder to go out on dates to certain places or be physically intimate with someone.

The good news is that, with careful planning, most of these practical issues can be overcome. For example, good communication is essential in any relationship and when people have difficulties in this area they can be supported to express themselves or what they want. Similarly, it is possible to go on dates to venues that have disabled access.

Another common issue arises when one person's attraction to someone else is not reciprocated. Not everyone we are attracted to is equally attracted to us. This is something that almost everyone on the planet will have experienced at one time or another and the truth is this can be painful. Being rejected is never nice, particularly when we have strong feelings for that person.

This predicament can be more pronounced for people with disabilities when they are attracted to people without disabilities, as they are more likely to be rejected.

In addition, disabled people will, by definition, differ from the mainstream and therefore are vulnerable to being stigmatised and prejudiced against. A social stigma is the negative attitude/behaviour directed towards people who differ from the perceived cultural norms. Because of their different abilities and appearance, disabled people are more likely to be a stigmatised group in Western societies and this will affect their ability to find a romantic partner. For example, research has shown that people often make judgements about someone's attractiveness based on what people can do and their general social status. Disabled people can be disadvantaged here due to lack of work and social opportunities.

Disabled people can also experience self-stigma and feel negatively towards themselves. This can be very painful and it is not uncommon for young people to react against this by wanting to have a relationship with a person without a disability (i.e a person in a less stigmatised group). The logic goes that if I have a relationship with someone without a disability, then I will be perceived more positively by other people. However, this person may be less inclined to have a relationship with a person with a lower social status who belongs to a stigmatised group. This mismatch can be difficult for the disabled person because it means their search for a partner will be much harder. The population of people who would want a relationship with them is smaller than the population of people they would want to have a relationship with and this can lead to a series of frustrations, anger and disappointments.

Finally, like the rest of the population, some disabled children will be attracted to people of the same sex. There is no evidence that the prevalence of same-sex relationships (i.e. homosexuality) is any higher or lower in disabled populations, so it is probably safe to assume that it is at a similar level. While the situation is improving, homosexuality is still a stigmatised issue in the UK and this is likely to present a disabled young person with yet another additional barrier to engaging in a same-sex relationship.

> Ismail is 16 years old and has a mild learning disability. He lives with his mother and younger brother. Ismail has good verbal communication and attends a local special school. Once a week his uncle takes him to a local community centre where he has become attracted to a girl who attends the same class. However, while she likes him as a friend, she is not interested in him romantically. Ismail is very upset by this and becomes quite obsessed by the girl, talking about her all the time. As her rejection continues, he becomes angry and shouts at her. This makes her cry and she doesn't want to be his friend anymore. But this only makes Ismail angrier. His mother doesn't know what to do and she finds it painful to see her son in such distress. She worries about the future for him.

What can we do?

People with disabilities have the same right and desire to have romantic relationships with other people as everyone else. The task therefore for families and wider support networks is to support them with this goal in safe and meaningful ways. There are a number of stages for supporting your child to have a relationship.

- Education: An essential starting point for all young people before beginning a relationship with someone is to understand their bodies, emotions and what a healthy relationship with someone should look like (i.e. how they should behave and what they can expect from a partner). There are a number of really useful resources and books for helping young people with this issue, which can be found at your local library or on the Internet.

- Opportunity: If your child says they want to have a relationship with someone but hasn't found anyone they are attracted to, they will need help finding a suitable partner. This can be done through attending social events, community groups or even online dating (however, be careful with online dating because how people present themselves online is often not accurate and this can open up the opportunity for a potentially abusive relationship).

- Support: If your child has met someone they are attracted to, they might need emotional and practical support. For example, they might need to be driven or helped to dress before meeting a potential partner for a date. Or they might need some guidance about what to say and how to have conversations while on a date. They might need guidance around appropriate social and sexual boundaries with their partner or how to manage their finances together. This list of things that people might need help with is potentially endless, but as a general principle it is safe to assume they will help with something. After all, we all need help from time to time. Therefore, to minimise the likelihood of something going wrong, it is a good idea to undertake an assessment of their needs with the person and openly plan how to meet them. This won't guarantee success, but it will help overcome any more obvious barriers and problems.

- Emotions: Romantic relationships will inevitably bring up all sorts of feelings and emotions, some of them positive and some negative. Being able to talk about how you feel and what you do and don't like is important in any relationship. This is why it is important to help people know what they are feeling and to express themselves clearly (see Section 6.2 for a discussion about how to increase your child's emotional literacy).

- Safety: People with disabilities can be more likely to be vulnerable to abusive relationships. There are likely to be a number of reasons for this. One might be that they do not understand what is happening and so they are more easily taken advantage of (e.g. their partner might misuse their finances). Another might be that their emotional vulnerability makes it hard to express their feelings (e.g. they may be so desperate for a relationship that they find it hard to say 'no' to their partner). We explored the issue of vulnerability to abuse in more detail in Section 6.1.

- Sexual health and reproduction: If your child is entering a sexual relationship with someone, they will need to be aware of the physical health issues associated with sexual intercourse – in particular the potential for disease and for pregnancy. This can be achieved by regularly checking in with their health, teaching them effective self-care and cleanliness skills and, if necessary, arranging visits to a suitably qualified health practitioner.

Resources

King, K. (2008) I Said No: *A Kid-to-Kid Guide to Keeping Your Private Parts Private*. Weaverville, CA: Boulden Publishing.

Mosley, J. and Grogan, R. (2008) *The Big Book of Calmers*. Trowbridge: Positive Press.

Chapter 7

RELATIONSHIPS

This chapter presents questions that families often ask about how to support their children's relationships, including friendships, romantic relationships and marriage.

7.1 How do I teach my child what makes a friend?

Forming and having friendships is important to all of us. We share our best times and worst times with our friends, and life is very lonely without them. Friendships provide us with a sense of connection, belonging, fun and joy. With friends, we know we matter to someone not just because we are part of the family or because they are paid. Friendships have ups and downs of course and, while some last a lifetime, others are brief and fleeting. But whatever their form and duration, they all matter.

DEFINITIONS

Friendship is defined as a relationship in which two or more people care about each other. It can mean different things to different people, of course, and there are no clearly defined rules for a friendship. But most friendships are based on trust, compassion and fun. We trust our friends, we care for them and actively seek to support them, and we enjoy their company. Some friendships are closer than others, depending on how connected we feel to someone and how much time we spend with them. Research shows we generally rate our wellbeing and happiness to be higher when we have good and close friendships. 'A friend is one that knows you as you are, understands where you have been, accepts what you have become, and still, gently allows you to grow.'

Most parents hope that their child will find at least one special friend and most also go through the heartache of seeing their children's attempts at friendships sometimes flourish and sometimes fail. Parents of children with intellectual disabilities often have some extra concerns about their child's ability to find a special friend and about their understanding of friendship. Children with intellectual disabilities can find it difficult to make and/or keep friends for different reasons, which might include the following:

- They are struggling to find a way to join in with others.

- They are struggling with understanding the differences between bullying and 'banter'.

- Other children seem to avoid them because of their behaviour or their difficulty sharing/taking turns.

- They consider someone to be a friend even if they have spoken to them once.

- They are not sure of the differences between a friend and a boyfriend/girlfriend.

Max is 6 years old and has autism. He desperately wants a friend but seems to find it difficult to get started with making friendships. His mum thinks that this is partly because he struggles to let other children choose games, or to let them lead in play. He also tends to avoid other children. His parents are concerned that he will feel lonely.

What's the issue?

It is not uncommon for children with an intellectual disability or a diagnosis of autism to seem quite happy playing alone, and they perhaps seem to prefer this to interacting in groups. However, in our experience, children like Max would often like to be able to play with others and develop friendships – they may just be unsure of how to do this or be overwhelmed by their experience of having to respond to complex social situations. One of the core difficulties that Max's mum has noticed for him is being able to let other children choose a game. Often children with a diagnosis of autism may need some support to see the wider benefits of allowing another child to choose a game (e.g. if the other child enjoys it, they may feel happy and be more likely to try things you want to do).

 What can we do?

1 Organise playdates

Evidence suggests that inviting one child at a time to play with your child gives children the best chance of developing friendships (Frankel 2010). This has to be regular contact to make enough of a difference.

Max's parents could give him some choice about whom he would like to invite home so that he is as motivated as possible. It could be another child from school or from a club he attends. If Max's parents don't pick him up from school, and therefore don't have opportunities to talk to other parents and arrange playdates, they could write a note or an invitation and ask the teacher to pass it on.

Before the playdate, Max's parents could help him to plan it and prepare him to understand what might help it to go smoothly. During the playdate they could make sure that his brothers and sisters are occupied elsewhere and limit access to things like technology, to encourage Max to play with interactive toys/games. It might be difficult if Max is used to spending time on technology on his own, to suddenly have this taken away from him when another child comes to play. His parents might need to set up regular expectations about how long he has on technology in an evening. His parents could help him get used to frequently playing one indoor and one outdoor game that is interactive so that he could successfully play with another child independently.

2 Teach your child about joining in and other skills

Friendship usually starts with play and requires the skills of joining in with play, maintaining interesting play, sharing, taking turns and resolving conflict. This is the same for all children, no matter what their level of communication. As children grow older, friendship is often based around conversation, and more sophisticated skills are required. Giving children a helping hand and explicitly teaching them these skills, rather than hoping they pick them up, can be a good foundation for the development of friendships.

Max may need some help to understand when to join in. His parents could teach him to watch other children, decide if he is interested in what they are doing and, if there is a 'pause' in the play, to try to join in. He might need help with asking to participate. It could help Max to have a 'script' or ways of joining in with other children – for example, by saying 'Do you need another person to play on your team?' or 'Wow that (toy) looks cool!' Helping Max to accept if someone doesn't want to play, or doesn't want to play at that moment, might also be important. Sometimes more sensitive children need help to understand that there can be multiple reasons why their attempt to join in with someone hasn't worked out. For example, it might be something they did (they might have asked at the wrong time) or it might be something to do with the other child (they might have wanted to play with their usual friends that day). Max's parents could remind him that someone will want to be his friend and it is important not to give up; everyone has ups and downs when trying to make friends.

3 Coach social skills before the playdate and in the moment

Before Max has a friend home to play, he might need support to understand the unwritten rules of friendship. His parents could help prepare him to know what is likely to happen and what would make his guest feel comfortable. For example, his parents could ask him to plan what to play, and how to ask his guest to choose what to play. They could help him learn the skills of managing conflict and planning ahead about how to handle this if it happens. Max might need help with knowing when to 'tell' on the friend to an adult (i.e. if someone is upset or hurt or if they have tried to work it out and can't) and when to try to resolve any conflict himself.

4 The friendship bench

Some of the schools we have worked with have introduced a 'friendship' bench. The idea is that if someone needs a friend, they can sit on the bench and other children and adults will know that child needs some help and support.

Figure 7.1 The 'friendship' bench

5 Pets and unconditional friendship

Many parents we have worked with have talked about their family pets providing 'unconditional' friendship and companionship to their children.

6 Who/what kind of person makes a good friend?

Sometimes children need some extra help to understand what makes a 'good' friend. As parents, you may have your own idea of what makes a good friend, based on your own experiences of friendship. Some of the resources at the end of the chapter have some worksheets to help children explore this concept. You can also make your own lists or social stories with children.

What makes a good friendship?

- Having fun together.

- Taking turns to lead or being equal.

- Letting each other have time with other friends.

- Working hard to make up if you fall out.

- Respecting each other's differences.

Often, children with intellectual disabilities or a diagnosis of autism may be drawn to either younger children or older children. This might be because younger children are at a more similar developmental level and enjoy playing similar games, or because older people are 'easier' to get on with and more accommodating of the child's wishes.

7 Teach them what bullying is

Some children may not realise or pick up on cues that they are being bullied, or that what they are doing is bullying. They may benefit from explicit teaching about what bullying is and the difference between banter and bullying.

WHAT IS BANTER?

'Banter' means making jokes or using words that are teasing but meant to be friendly; they happen as a one off.

WHAT IS BULLYING?

Bullying is being unkind to others. It is using words to hurt someone's feelings, or hurt someone's body. Bullying may be done over and over again. It may make you feel uncomfortable or upset. Bullying can happen to anyone and it can be done by anyone.

7.2 My daughter's got a boyfriend/ girlfriend, what's going on?

DEFINITIONS

In everyday language 'boyfriend' or 'girlfriend' are the words we use to describe a regular romantic companion. Usually there is a sexual dimension to these relationships, though not always. The words boyfriend and girlfriend usually indicate a more short-term relationship than other titles like husband, wife or partner. Key to a boyfriend/girlfriend relationship is the idea of romance, companionship and sexual attraction. While having a boyfriend/ girlfriend is usually desired and quite natural for young people, in fact they need to learn a lot of skills to have a successful relationship.

A high proportion of teenagers and adults with intellectual disabilities want to be in romantic relationships. They generally want the same thing as everyone else – to date, to be romantic, to have sex, to have the choice to marry and to have the choice to have children. While these desires are quite natural for everyone, they can be worrying for parents and carers of disabled children. 'What will a romantic relationship involve?' 'Where will it lead?' 'Can they cope?' and 'Will they be safe?' are just some of the questions that can come up.

For these (and many other) reasons, it can feel much easier to ignore the issue of romantic relationships, in the hope that your child is 'not interested'. The problem with this approach is that it is unlikely that just because your child isn't talking about relationships, they aren't curious about them. There is a chance, then, that they might make some poor choices about whom they want to have a relationship with or how to behave in a relationship.

Before non-disabled young people reach the age when they want to have romantic relationships, they have usually had a lot of experience in managing friendships and everyday relationships. By the time they start having boyfriends and girlfriends, parents are usually confident that they can manage what it involves. If not, they will usually talk to their child about the issues and look to skill them up quickly. Once this has happened, the young person will go off and manage their relationships themselves as they gradually move into adulthood and full independence.

But even when the young person is sensible and well informed about how to behave in romantic relationships, this is a very anxious time for parents and carers. And this anxiety is usually all the greater for parents and carers of disabled children, particularly in relation to their emotional and physical safety. We think that providing children with support to develop fun, safe and healthy romantic relationships is a more effective way to keep them safe. This is all the more important for children with intellectual disabilities because their more limited understanding of the world means they can be more vulnerable to making bad decisions. Teaching children with intellectual disabilities relationships skills will usually take longer and there will need to be more opportunities for practice, but this doesn't change the underlying reason for doing it. Your child may need more time to learn about:

- communicating in a romantic relationship; making decisions about intimacy and personal limits

- sex, contraception, sexually transmitted infections (STIs) and pregnancy

- the difference between love and a crush.

Alice is 16 and has a diagnosis of autism and a mild intellectual disability. She told her mum that she has a boyfriend at school. Her favourite soap currently has a storyline that involves a teenager having unprotected sex with her boyfriend. Her mum is worried that she will want to copy this and carry it out in her relationship as quickly as it seems to happen on TV. She is wondering whether to tell her daughter that she is not allowed to have a boyfriend yet.

What's the issue?

Alice, like other teenagers, is developing her sexuality and her interest in romantic relationships. She wants to explore this side of her life, just like everyone else, and at the same time she may need some extra help to develop her relationship skills and knowledge of sex and consent. Her mum is concerned that Alice is taking some of the storylines from her favourite soap opera quite literally, and not realising that it can take time for relationships to develop in real life. It is not uncommon for parents to give young people the message that relationships are 'off limits', as a way of protecting them. While this might appear to deal with the issue, in our experience it rarely does because the young person still has an interest in the area. Without accurate information and the development of key social skills, the young person is vulnerable to behaving in ways that can cause them problems further down the line.

What can we do?

1 Talk about the stepping stones in relationships

In our experience, it is helpful to set aside a significant amount of time to talk to young people about the stepping stones in relationships – from first seeing someone you fancy or someone you have a crush on, to becoming friends, asking them out, getting to know each other, kissing and developing sexual relationships.

Each step along the way allows for discussion about:

- the social and sexual 'rules'
- the normal feelings that everyone experiences
- dilemmas that might come up and choices that can be made
- skills for handling rejection and/or conflict
- skills for building positive and fun relationships.

For example, as a first step, Alice's parents could ask her what she thinks it means to be boyfriend and girlfriend. They could let her know that it is normal to have feelings of fancying someone, wanting to be close to someone and to start a sexual relationship. They could talk to her about checking out that the person she fancies is old enough to be in a sexual relationship, if that is what she wants. She may also need help to think about whether the person wants the same as her and if they agree to it. Sometimes young people need a bit of help to understand the differences between liking someone, loving someone and having a crush on someone. If the other person does not reciprocate their feelings, they may benefit from knowing how to handle this. Below is an example of a social story about managing crushes:

Crushes

When people have romantic feelings for someone else we usually call this a crush.

Crushes make us think about someone a lot and daydream about them. They might make us feel happy, nervous, excited or silly.

Crushes are temporary, they do not last forever.

When the person we have a crush on does not feel the same way, or does not want to be in a relationship, we have to respect that.

Respecting the other person means that we do not talk to them about it or touch them.

If we can make ourselves busy by doing things with other people, the crush will go away.

Alice's parents may need to teach her the concepts of 'public' and 'private' and be explicit about where it is okay and not okay to kiss someone, and where it is okay and not okay to have sex with someone.

Alice's parents might benefit from watching her favourite soap with her – to use the storyline as a way of opening up conversations about what's happening and the choices the characters could make at different points.

If her relationship progresses, her parents may benefit from talking to her about the next steps in making choices about a sexual relationship.

2 Answer questions honestly and provide information about sexual relationships

In our experience parents think that because their child isn't asking questions about their body, relationships or sex, they aren't yet ready for those things. This may be the case, but very often children are incredibly curious about these experiences; they just don't know how to ask or to start a conversation, or may have missed out on opportunities to talk about these things with peers.

Alice's parents may feel that she is not ready for a sexual relationship yet, but she is certainly showing a lot of curiosity. The most effective way of helping her to make some smart choices about keeping herself safe and being happy in a relationship is to give her some information about sex, consent, contraception and STIs. Most parents feel uncomfortable talking about these issues, and most hope that they will only have to have the conversation once. However, having a one-off conversation is rarely enough for young people with intellectual disabilities. We would recommend asking school to help develop a programme of work for your child, so that they can help reinforce the messages and information that you want them to have.

Young people may need to know that when two people (age 16 or over) start to feel sexy, they may want to kiss, touch each other, take their clothes off and touch their private parts.

This is okay if they both agree and are in private. To check that they both agree they can ask each other if it is okay, and if the other person wants to do it (consent). Usually, there are changes to your body that happen when you start to feel sexy with someone – for example, a man's penis will start to go hard (an erection). Before two people have sexual intercourse, they need to both check that they agree, and to talk about contraception. This is so that they can make some choices to stay healthy (and not get STIs) and to stop them from getting pregnant if they are not yet ready to have a baby.

Understanding the choices that can be made about contraception can take some planning. Young people need to know how to use different methods of contraception, and where to get them from. Young people with intellectual disabilities may need to practise the skills of buying condoms or arranging to get them from the school nurse or GP. This might include skills in managing money, or making appointments.

We have recommended some resources at the end of this chapter, which can help you talk about sex with your son or daughter. It is likely that young people will need this information to be simplified, given in small chunks and repeated.

3 Help your child learn relationship skills directly

Giving people information is a good first step, but often it is inadequate for teaching people how to behave in everyday situations. It might be that your child needs direct skills training to learn how to behave in a relationship. The best way to do this is with roleplay with their peers. Often local colleges will run relationship classes that involve roleplay and this is a fun and natural place to learn these skills. But if this isn't available, you might need to organise something yourself with friends or someone else you know with similarly aged disabled children. You can then set up scenarios and script how the young people should behave in different situations. Different topics might include:

- asking someone on a date

- how to behave on a date

- talking about feelings

- dealing with conflict and disagreement

- kissing and sexual boundaries (including consent).

Practising these skills directly, and ideally with other young disabled children, will give your child the best chance of knowing how to behave in a romantic relationship.

4 Talk about issues of consent and ending relationships

As well as teaching children about the issue of starting romantic relationships, it can also be important to teach them about how to end a relationship that they do not want to be in, or how to cope if the other person ends a relationship.

Alice's parent could talk to her about what she could do if someone wants a relationship and/or sex with her but she does not agree. They could practise her saying 'no' and asking for help from someone she trusts. They could reinforce that it is her right to choose what to do, and that she might have lots of different feelings (e.g. anger, fear), which would be quite normal.

Alice's parents could talk to her about what she could do if her boyfriend decides he does not want to be in a relationship with her, or if he does not want to kiss, touch or have sex with her. They could talk about how she might feel if that happens, and how it is normal to feel hurt and upset for a little while. These feelings won't last forever, and she can use some skills to help her cope with them. For example, she could talk to a friend or her family, she could do something fun, watch a favourite film or listen to her favourite music.

Finally, Alice's parents could support her to know that relationships can be fun and healthy. Many relationships are not always easy and people can fall out and argue. This can be okay, as long as people feel happy in their relationship most of the time, and feel good about themselves. When arguments happen, it can be a good thing to 'repair' the relationship and practise apologising. We cannot make other people accept our apology but we will know we have tried to fix it. This can sometimes make relationships even stronger.

7.3 Will my child ever be able to get married?

Marriage is perhaps the most important civil institution in human societies. It is central to how we make public and permanent commitments to the people we most care about. Marriage can be considered a symbol of love, commitment and family, so for these reasons it is valued highly by people and is something they often aspire to. People with intellectual disabilities are no different in this regard and many will hope to one day get married.

DEFINITIONS

Legally marriage is the socially recognised contract between two people that establishes rights and obligations between them and provides the basis for living together and having a family. But marriage is much more than just a legal contract. It is the focal point for romantic love, and wedding ceremonies are talked about as one of the most important events across all human societies. Because marriage is intended to be the union of two people forever, it involves making the deep commitment to do what it takes to make it a success. These are public, profound and lasting vows that set marriage apart from other relationships. This doesn't make marriage easy, of course, and no marriage is free of conflict and tension.

The United Nations Convention on the Rights of Persons with Disabilities says that people with intellectual disabilities have the right to get married, have children and have a sexual relationship. In the UK, this is supported by policy which states that people with intellectual disabilities should have the chance to have relationships if they want to.

Legally, if people with intellectual disabilities have the capacity to consent to marriage according to the Mental Capacity Act (2005) principles, and are of a legal age to do so, they are permitted to marry and should be supported to make their own choices about this. Services and families often find themselves negotiating a dilemma between wanting to empower young people and support their rights, whilst also protecting them from exploitation or harm.

> Ali and Simon are both 18 years old. They met at college and have been in a relationship for a year. They have been talking about getting married soon. Ali and Simon both have intellectual disabilities but Ali's parents feel that Simon has more power within the relationship because his independence skills are ahead of Ali's. They are concerned that their daughter may not understand what it means to be married and, though they are happy for them to be girlfriend and boyfriend, they worry that they are 'letting Simon take advantage' of her if they marry.

 What's the issue?

Following the principles of the Mental Capacity Act (2005), for a person to have the capacity to make a decision about marriage, they need to have an understanding of what marriage is, what a husband/wife is and understand that sexual activity is likely to be expected within marriage. The person also needs to have the capacity to consent to sexual activity. They need to understand what sex is, that sex without contraception could lead to STIs and/or pregnancy and that they have a right to say 'no' to sex. The person needs to be able to communicate their decisions, though this does not necessarily need to be verbally.

Arranged marriage is where the families of both people make arrangements for the marriage, but the individuals concerned consent to go ahead with it and accept the arrangements or not. The same principles apply here, in that if both individuals have the capacity to consent to and accept the marriage arranged for them, and both are of a legal age to marry, they have a right to make this decision.

A forced marriage is where one or both individuals do not or cannot consent to the marriage, but it goes ahead 'under duress' (Forced Marriage Unit 2009). It is illegal and, if you suspect it might be happening to a young person, it is important to act in accordance with child protection protocols and to seek advice from the Forced Marriage Unit before contacting anyone else. Most often, parents who force their children into marriage do so because they want to protect them and provide them with care and financial security in the future. They may also want to preserve cultural traditions. Nonetheless, there is no justification for forcing someone to marry.

 What can we do?

1 Talk to your child about their views of marriage

Ali's parents could talk to her about her view of marriage, her relationship and her hopes for the future. They could try to find out more about her understanding of what it means to be married, what a wife is and how being a wife is different to being a girlfriend or friend. If there are gaps in her understanding, they could support her to learn about marriage and different types of relationships.

Ali's parents could talk to her about her feelings for her boyfriend and committing to the relationship in the long term. They could check out whether she knows she can say 'no' to marriage if she wants to. As they are concerned about the power differences in the relationship, they may want to check out what she thinks would happen if she said 'no' to marriage.

2 Support your child emotionally

It may be that your child cannot find a suitable partner for marriage or in all likelihood may never be able to get married due to their limited mental capacity. If that is the case, they may feel frustrated, angry, confused or sad. These are difficult feelings and without any help they may be expressed as behaviour that is challenging.

The first thing to do when supporting your child with difficult feelings is to openly accept them. This validates what they are experiencing and shows your child that it is possible to accept them and not be overwhelmed by them. This won't be easy for you as facing negative feelings isn't nice, but it is valuable for your child to see that you can face these feelings yourself.

The second thing is to speak (or use signs or pictures) about what your child is feeling. This provides a language to understand what they are experiencing and enables them to talk about the world inside their skin and to express their emotions in healthy ways. These are the same principles as set out in Section 6.2 on emotional literacy.

3 Support their understanding of marriage and consent

Teach about options

Ali may benefit from some education around her options for the future, and the range of choices she could make. For example, she might want to know that she could make a choice to live with Simon without being married. She could live separately with her family or with a personal assistant, and get married to Simon later on in her life. Alternatively, she could choose to marry Simon.

Teach the right to refuse

If Ali has difficulty making decisions about her own life, it might be helpful to think about where she has the most power, and in which relationships she feels she is most able to give her opinion and make some choices – is this different in her relationship with Simon?

LETTING GO

Ali's parents are at a transition point themselves – the psychological process of 'letting go' means giving up some control over their daughter's life and choices, and supporting her to take some 'safe risks'. That is not an easy task for any parent, and separation for parents of children with disabilities is often a more difficult task in balancing protection with stepping back.

4 Consider asking for help with a Mental Capacity Act assessment

Ali's parents may already have an understanding of whether she has the capacity to consent to sexual activity. If she has not had an opportunity to access SRE, they may wish to support her with this, or ask her college to.

If Ali's parents are still concerned that she may not have the mental capacity to consent to marriage, they could ask for further support from the local Community Learning Disability Team, and they can speak to their GP about accessing this support.

7.4 How much choice and control should I give my child?

Growing up involves children progressively learning more and more skills as they become more independent. And as children grow, so too must adults gradually let go, little by little and step by step. The business of growing up, and of parents letting children grow up, usually happens one small step at a time. Babies move from being fed to feeding themselves, from a cot to a bed, from being with you all the time to attending nursery... this carries on all the way up to puberty when children often take bigger leaps away from you towards their friends, and a more independent life. The process of children exploring and separating happens in a dance, with parents remaining present, but letting go, in parallel. However, the process of letting go emotionally and physically can be more complicated for parents of children with disabilities, and puberty can be a time when feelings have to be faced on your part as well as your child's.

DEFINITIONS

Right from the moment children are born they are learning about the world. Research has shown, for instance, that day-old newborn babies learn to recognise and respond to their parents' faces. From that moment on, children learn more and more skills and with this they want to do more and more things. This is all quite natural but can also be a source of conflict when what they want is different from what their parents want. This challenge starts when children are infants and is usually most pronounced when children reach adolescence and are on the cusp of adulthood.

Some young people may be able to indicate when they want space, or when they want others to help them with tasks that you previously helped with, like dressing or intimate care. But for children with physical and intellectual disabilities, separation often has to be initiated and planned by parents. They may need you to let go of their hand first.

Alice is 15 years old. She has quadriplegic cerebral palsy and an intellectual disability. She can communicate verbally and goes to a mainstream school. Alice is growing up. She has started her periods and has a grown-up body. Alice would like to have a boyfriend. She will always need some help to manage her personal care and to access the community because her mobility is very limited. She has started to say she doesn't want to go to school when she has her period as she doesn't want anyone to have to help her change her pad. She has been asking whether she can go to the cinema with friends without her parents and feels that her friends can help manage her wheelchair. In the mornings she has been a bit irritated with her father when he helps her with getting dressed. He feels frustrated and realises that his daughter is growing up, but doesn't know what to do because she is also dependent on his care. He worries that she might be vulnerable to abuse by carers, or that her friends may not be responsible enough to support her without an adult.

What's the issue?

Alice's parents are trying to negotiate both a parent and carer role at the same time, and Alice is trying to work out how to grow up and separate from her parents whilst depending on their help. Alice may need more help to separate than other young people without disabilities. There are not many things that she can keep private as she needs help with intimate care and managing things like her periods. She may feel more comfortable having help from her parents than anyone else, as this is familiar and safe, yet at the same time, she may want some physical separation from them.

What can we do?

1 Think about who provides personal care

If we give young people an opportunity to choose who provides personal care as they grow up, we show them that they can have some control over their body and their privacy. Developing an intimate care plan can be a way to structure conversations about what kind of help a young person wants and from whom. This might require setting up support systems and personal assistants.

2 Develop your child's support network

Young people naturally tend to turn away from parents towards friendships at puberty. For some young people, these opportunities for friendships might need to be initiated and carefully managed by parents. But beware! It is easy for social opportunities for young people with intellectual disabilities to become institutionalised. The 'stay up late campaign' has emphasised the rights of people with intellectual disabilities to stay up past the usual hours of support workers/personal assistants. They want to be able to go to concerts and to stay out past 9pm just like everyone else.

Alice's parents may not be happy for her to go out with her peers as they may be concerned about asking her friends to take responsibility for her physical support needs. However, Alice probably doesn't want her parents tagging along. Another compromise might be for Alice to have a personal assistant whom she sees as more similar to herself, to support her while she joins in ordinary opportunities with friends. Some flexibility about support hours will probably help Alice have as ordinary a life as possible for a disabled teenager.

3 Increase functional independence skills

Many parents want education to focus on functional skills – it is much more important for them that their child leaves school being able to manage their own toileting needs, communicate about their feelings and organise outings with friends. Being clear about this at your child's annual school review is really important, if this is also important to your child.

4 Remember that worrying about the future is normal

How children grow and develop, and whether they are able to have an independent life, are things that all parents think about and worry about. As professionals we don't want to offer parents false hope or take away hope about what your child is likely to achieve. Sometimes children surprise us. Most of the time, all we can do is go along the journey with children, with some awareness that we may need to keep our expectations fluid. This doesn't mean simply 'hoping for the best'; neither does it mean 'throwing them in at the deep end' to get used to the 'real world'. We can put things in place to offer children the chance of having an ordinary life, and sometimes this requires extraordinary support systems and services. Starting off with extra support is often necessary for children not to experience failing or being 'not good enough'. Adjusting this support as they do develop skills, and allowing them to take some risks is also part of growing up.

5 Pay attention to the old feelings that come up

You might be thinking 'but I assumed I'd do it for him forever' or 'she is more vulnerable than other young people and not ready to handle the risks'.

Letting go is about letting go of control, and that is scary. It is not the same as leaving your child without support. Letting go and letting them have control over their own life might be about increasing your child's support networks and working on their functional daily living skills, social skills and relationship skills. It might be about making a deliberate choice to let others help care for them, knowing that as you get older yourself, this is going to be necessary.

There are things that can get in the way of letting go. Old feelings can get in the way. If early on, you had to hold on to them tightly because you thought your child wouldn't survive, it would not be surprising if letting go later on felt scarier than it would otherwise.

What you can do is simply recognise that the old feelings, and particularly fear, are there. If you recognise that these feelings are influencing your interaction with your child, in the moment, you have a choice about how to respond to your child and how much to let fear influence your decisions.

Resources
Social skills

Kelly, A. (2013) *Talkabout for Children 3: Developing Friendship Skills.* Milton Keynes: Speechmark Publishing Ltd.

Madorsky Elman, N. and Kennedy Moore, E. (2004) *The Unwritten Rules of Friendship: Simple Strategies to Help Your Child Make Friends.* London: Little Brown and Company.

Sexual and romantic relationships

Jason's Private World or *Kylie's Private World* DVDs; available at www.lifesupportproductions.co.uk/jpwdvd.php, accessed 9 April 2016.

Kerr-Edwards, L. and Scott, L. (2007) *Talking Together About Contraception: A Practical Resource for Parents and Staff Working with Young People with Learning Disabilities.* London: Family Planning Association.

Kerr-Edwards, L. and Scott, L. (2010) *Talking Together About Sex and Relationships: A Practical Resource for Schools and Parents Working with Young People with Learning Disabilities.* London: Family Planning Association.

Leeds Nursing (2009) *Puberty and sexuality for children and young people with a learning disability (a supporting document for national curriculum objectives).* Leeds: The Children's Learning Disability Nursing Team. www.leeds.gov.uk/docs/Puberty-and-Sexuality-Pack-Session1-4.pdf

MarriageUnited Nations Conventions on the Rights of Persons with Disabilities; available at www.un.org/disabilities/convention/conventionfull.shtml, accessed 28 January 2016.

Chapter 8

YOUNG PEOPLE, SEX AND THE LAW

This chapter presents questions that families ask in relation to their young people, sex and the law.

8.1 Will my son/daughter be legally allowed to have a sexual relationship at 16?

Tina is 17 and has a diagnosis of moderate intellectual disability. She has a boyfriend who is thought to be 'vulnerable' but who does not have an intellectual disability. She has told her parents that she and her boyfriend want to have sex and get married.

The legal age of consent to sex in the UK is 16 for men and women, for heterosexual and homosexual relationships. It is no longer assumed that because someone has an intellectual disability they should be prevented from making a choice about having a sexual relationship once they reach 16. This is also the case for people with severe intellectual disabilities.

Tina's parents and the people who support her might need to consider the following issues when thinking about whether she should be prevented or protected from having a sexual relationship.

- Does Tina (and her boyfriend) have the *capacity to consent* to sex?

- Is Tina *able to consent* to sex willingly and free from coercion?

These issues are important because the Sexual Offences Act 2003 (Section 74) (HMSO 2003) states that 'a person consents if s/he agrees by choice and has the freedom and capacity to make that choice'.

1 The capacity to consent to sex

The first question – 'Does Tina have the capacity to consent to sex?' – needs to be considered in relation to the Mental Capacity Act (DH, 2005) in the UK.

The Mental Capacity Act (2005) states that a person should only be considered unable to make a decision if s/he is unable to carry out any of the following steps in decision making:

- understand the information relevant to the decision

- retain that information

- use or weigh that information as part of the process of making the decision

- communicate his or her decision (whether by talking, sign language or other means).

If Tina does have some sexual knowledge, if she can retain this knowledge, and if she is able to communicate her decision about whether she does or does not want to have sex (verbally or in other ways), then we would assume that she does have capacity.

Tina needs to know what sex is and understand that it can lead to STIs, HIV and/or pregnancy. She needs to understand that HIV can lead to death.

If Tina does not demonstrate sexual knowledge, her support system would be expected to provide her with information and education (e.g. via school/college/sexual health services), and then she would need to demonstrate that she can retain this knowledge over a period of time.

It is important to remember that, whilst the Mental Capacity Act can act as a protective measure in ensuring that people with intellectual disabilities are not abused, we also need to ensure that the standards we expect of young people are not more restrictive than for people without intellectual disabilities. For example, we need to make sure that we do not expect young people with intellectual disabilities to have extensive sexual knowledge, over and above what we would expect of young people/teenagers without intellectual disabilities.

2 Consenting to sex free from coercion

The second question – 'Can Tina consent to sex willingly and free from coercion?' – means that she must be able to voluntarily decide with whom she wishes to have or not have sex; she must be reasonably protected from physical or psychological harm and not be taken advantage of by another person.

This means that it is possible for a young person with an intellectual disability to be able to consent to sex with one person and not another – for example, if they are intimidated or feel threatened in a relationship, it is unlikely that they will be able to consent willingly. The Sexual Offences Act (2003) has a section that is relevant to carer relationships and which makes it illegal for people who are caring for people with intellectual disabilities to have sex with them.

Tina's family or carers may have some concerns about the power differences within her relationship and may feel concerned that she will be pressured to have a sexual relationship.

Tina's parents could help her to know about her rights to say 'no' or 'yes' in relation to decisions about sex. They can support her in everyday life to have the confidence and power to make decisions for herself. They can respect her choice to say 'no' or 'yes' in relation to other decisions. Her parents could support her to develop other relationships in her life and feel good about herself generally. If they are still concerned, Tina's parents could ask for some support from the learning disability team, to help assess her capacity to consent in that particular relationship.

Please see Chapter 6 Section 6.1 (on protecting your child from abuse).

8.2 What happens if my child exposes themselves or masturbates in public?

Mohammed is 15 and has a diagnosis of autism spectrum disorder and severe intellectual disability. His parents say that he has started to masturbate a lot of the time and often has his hands down his trousers, even when they go out to the shops.

The Sexual Offences Act (2003) has an offence of 'exposure', which means that someone has intentionally exposed their genitals, intending for someone to see them and to cause alarm or distress.

If your child accidentally exposes their genitals in public (e.g. if they come out of the toilet and have forgotten to fasten their trousers, or if they strip off their clothes because they are distressed or overwhelmed by social experiences), this would not be considered intentional.

Mohammed's behaviour is much more problematic. It is possible that he has not learnt the rules of 'public' and 'private' and so is responding to his emerging sexual feelings and experiences as they occur. Though he may not be deliberately intending for others to see him, he may cause members of the public alarm or distress. In Chapter 5, Section 5.2, we offer some ideas about how you might be able to handle this with your child if it does happen.

8.3 Can I help my son/daughter access a disability sex worker?

Hugo is 16 and has quadriplegic cerebral palsy. He wants to have a sexual relationship but feels that he won't ever be able to find a girlfriend who accepts his disability. He has told his parents that he does not want his disability to stop him having the same experiences as other young people and he has asked them to help him practically by organising contact with a disability sex worker.

At the time of writing this book, in the UK it is not illegal for a person to pay for the sexual services of someone unless that person is under 18; unless the person is being exploited by a third party; or if someone solicits their services in a public place.

However, Section 39 of the Sexual Offences Act (2003) relates to care workers and states that it is illegal for care workers to cause or incite another person to engage in sexual activity. This means that if anyone providing care to Hugo supported him with his request through making practical arrangements for him (e.g. booking the sex worker, driving him to the appointment), they could be considered to be causing or inciting him to engage in sexual activity.

Although the section may not have intended to refer to a person's parents as care workers, the definition means that they could be included. Although the interpretation of the law is debated, care workers and parents in the UK could be open to prosecution if they support a young person with an intellectual disability to access a sex worker, even if it was the person's idea and request (for further information about these issues, see Jones 2012).

That is not to say that it is impossible for a young person to access a sex worker or disability sex worker. If the young person was over 16, if they had the capacity to consent and did consent, and if they could make the arrangements independently, this would not be considered illegal. It is important to note that the issue of capacity needs to relate to the specific relationship with a sex worker. This means that the person would need to understand what will and will not be expected within the relationship (e.g. expectation that a condom will be used, and that the relationship will not continue afterwards).

These complicated issues have been explored in films and documentaries, for example, *Come as You Are* (2011) and *Otto: Love, Lust and Las Vegas* (BBC3 2009).

8.4 How do I stop my child from accessing illegal sites or doing anything illegal online?

James is 17 years old. He has a mild intellectual disability. James' parents are worried that he is accessing pornography online. They worry that he will not be able to distinguish between legal and illegal porn and this could have very serious consequences.

In the UK it is illegal to possess pornographic material that is extreme (e.g. depicting rape), obscene (e.g. depicting sex with animals) or depicts indecent images of children. It is very unlikely that James would come across child pornography by accident as it is not advertised. Most adult pornography sites also operate with age restrictions and ask young people to verify their age first. However, some websites do not operate with age restrictions and it could happen that James accesses an illegal pornography site, with or without realising.

It is for you as parents to ensure there are appropriate safeguards on the computers and tablets to which your child has access. Remember, you would not let your child go out in the community without first teaching them about road safety and 'stranger' danger. The Internet is no different. It is our responsibility to teach children how to stay safe online and in online relationships.[1]

Young people, like James, who are accessing pornography online need to be aware of the potential consequences in relation to the law.

---

1 There are a number of websites that provide information for parents: www.saferinternet.org.uk, https://esafety.gov.au/about-the-office/role-of-the-office, www.parentsprotect.co.uk

8.5 Can my daughter be given contraceptive advice without my knowledge?

Young people of 16 or over can obtain contraceptive advice and treatment without parental consent. Doctors can also provide advice and treatment to under 16s, if they believe that the young person is mature enough to understand. This is the same for young people with intellectual disabilities. However, in our experience, it is very unusual that young people with intellectual disabilities are offered the same opportunities for contraceptive advice or treatment. More often, decisions are made for them about whether they should be given contraception (such as the depo-provera injection). This should only be done in a young person's best interests if they are considered not to have capacity in accordance with the Mental Capacity Act (2005).

Young women with intellectual disabilities should be assumed to have capacity to make their own decisions about when to start and/or stop contraception, unless there is a good reason to consider they require a capacity assessment. If a young person does not have capacity, but would do if they were given adequate and accessible information, this must be provided.

Chapter 9

RELATIONSHIPS AND SEX EDUCATION

This chapter presents a relationships and sex education (RSE) programme for young people with intellectual disabilities. It is a flexible programme that can be tailored for your child's needs.

An RSE programme for young people with intellectual disabilities

Sexual rights

The programme described here is underpinned by the idea that people with intellectual disabilities have a right to experience and express their sexuality in safe and appropriate ways. The rights of people with intellectual disabilities to be sexual were first set out byAnn Craft (1987) in three main principles:

- The right to know.

- The right to be sexual.

- The right not to be sexually abused.

However, because many young people with more profound intellectual disabilities will not have the capacity to consent to sexual relationships under the Mental Capacity Act (2005) (see Chapter 8), it can be easy to overlook the issue of sexuality in general. For instance, we might struggle to see how RSE teaching would be be relevant to children with only limited language, or how it can be adapted to meet a young person's specific physical needs.

Our approach is based on the concept of sexuality in its broadest sense. Young people may not enter into sexual relationships, but their bodies still grow and develop just like everyone else's. They may not always be able to express themselves or understand fully their social setting, but we believe they will have the same basic underlying biology, desires and emotions. When they grow into adults, they will develop a sexual dimension to who they are. And like the rest of us, for some people this will be more important and for others it will be less important, which means a one size fits all approach may not be adequate. We need to tailor our support to each individual's needs and desires. The premise of this book, therefore, is that, just like the rest of society, people with intellectual disabilities have the right to be sexual, to express their gender, and to have sexual contact with others according to their level of interest and ability.

The rest of this chapter will set out how to plan and deliver an RSE programme for young people with intellectual disabilities.

Intimate care plans

Intimate and personal care is often provided at home and school every day for children and young people with multiple disabilities. As much as possible, the voice of the young person should guide this process. We should enable them to make decisions and choices about what is happening to empower them to be in control of their lives and confident enough to say what they do and do not like. Developing intimate care plans in collaboration with young people is a starting point for supporting them to develop relationship and communication skills. The following box describes an exercise that encourages discussion about the importance of your role in providing intimate care.

Intimate care is often focused on continence, washing and hygiene. A greater level of independence in toileting is often considered a key outcome for children and parents, leading to increased self-confidence and social opportunities. It is a place where young people can be taught independence skills, communication skills and decision making skills. It is a place in which young people receive messages about their bodies, their rights to privacy and their rights not to be sexually abused.

The intimate care plans can be used to focus on helping young people to make choices about how care is provided, how much they can do for themselves and how you can both communicate about what's happening. The plans also enable young people and carers to agree safe practices. For example, it is possible that sexual arousal may occur for some young people during intimate care, as a result of physical responses to their genitals being cleaned. In order to keep young people safe, the care plan addresses how this might be minimised and the expected response from carers. Being clear about how to respond in these situations also helps carers with their own emotional reactions as it will normalise and explain what is happening in an open and upfront way.

Reflecting on your experience of intimate care

Going to the dentist exercise

When you visit the dentist, what are the thoughts and feelings that come up for you when you are in the dentist chair, unable to speak with your mouth open?

What makes going to the dentist easier for you?

What could your dentist do to make you feel more comfortable and less anxious?

How would you feel if the dentist talked to her assistant over the top of you?

What do you think might be important to your children when you provide personal care?

Individually tailored RSE programmes

In order to be effective, each young person's RSE programme will need to be individually designed to reflect their personal needs. Therefore, the information set out in Table 9.1 is presented in general form and can be adapted to the young person's level of intellectual ability. The table presents the core topics that could be covered within an RSE teaching programme, with ideas for exercises and recommendations for resources. While individual sections can be completed in isolation, we advise seeing this programme as a cumulative model, so that each stage builds on the next, and skills are practised over and over.

Table 9.1 A model RSE programme for young people with intellectual disabilities

Topic	Aims/targets	Resources	Skills and knowledge
Feelings and self-identity	To develop emotional literacy skills To develop positive self-identity and self-esteem	Positive images of people with disabilities Photographs and pictures of different people Stories Symbols and photographs representing different feelings Dunn Buron, K. and Curtis, M. (2012) *The Incredible 5-Point Scale: Assisting Students in Understanding Social Interactions and Controlling Their Emotional Responses*. Lenexa, KS: AAPC Publishing Kelly, A. (2011) *Talkabout for Children 1: Developing Self-Awareness and Self-Esteem*. Milton Keynes: Speechmark Publishing Kelly, A. (2011) *Talkabout Cards: Self Awareness Activities*. Milton Keynes: Speechmark Publishing	**Recognising and naming feelings** Help your child to learn words/signs for basic feelings (happy, sad, angry) and teach them to label their feelings in the moment – see Chapter 6, Section 6.2. Use storybooks to help children recognise characters' feelings. **Communicating feelings** Practise communicating using words/signs/symbols through roleplay, using a mirror and in the moment – see Chapter 7. Remember to share how you are feeling and why. **Understanding and using body language** Practise different facial expressions in the mirror. Use roleplay, TV clips and stories to identify how people are feeling from their body language. **Knowing what I like and don't like** Make an 'All about me book' with photographs of your child's likes and dislikes (food, activities, preferred ways of interacting and communicating, important routines). Add to the book over time. Encourage children to express whether they like or dislike experiences/activities/clothes/foods, etc. **Knowing what kind of person I want to be** Teach values vocabulary (e.g. kind, bossy, helpful, fair, jolly, etc.) and let children know when they have acted in line with those values. **Knowing what I am good at and what I need help with** Help children to map out: • things I can do on my own • things I need some help with • things I need others to do for me. **Responding to feelings** Help children to develop a plan and learn positive ways to respond to their emotions: • When I am calm I can… • When I am angry I can… • When I am upset I can… **Understanding sexual feelings** Teach children that sexual feelings are normal, especially during puberty, and they can make you want to be close to someone or to touch your body or the other person's body. Some children might need help to know how to respond to these feelings – for example, what to do in public, such as thinking of something else (distraction) or moving away from the person to whom they are attracted.

Topic	Aims/targets	Resources	Skills and knowledge
Body parts, body changes, awareness of gender, public and private concepts	To be able to name body parts To make choices about how I express gender To understand 'public' and 'private' concepts To understand how my body will change	Bodyworks: A resource for learners with PMLD: (email: admin@oakfield.nottingham.sch.uk) Anatomically correct dolls (Body Sense: www.bodysense.org.uk) Images of the lifecycle: Reynolds, K. (2015) *What's Happening to Ellie? A Book about Puberty for Girls and Young Women with Autism and Related Conditions*. London: Jessica Kingsley Publishers Parker, V. (2007) *The Little Book of Growing Up*. London: Hodder Objects of reference, e.g. shaving kit, sanitary towel, male/female clothes Makaton sex education book of signs and symbols (The Makaton Charity: email: info@makaton.org) Photographs of the young person over their lifecycle King, K. (2008) *I Said No: A Kid-to-Kid Guide to Keeping Your Private Parts Private*. Weaverville, CA: Boulden Publishing Leeds Nursing (2009) *Puberty and sexuality for children and young people with a learning disability (a supporting document for national curriculum objectives)*. Leeds: The Children's Learning Disability Nursing Team, available at www.leeds.gov.uk/docs/Puberty-and-Sexuality-Pack-Session1-4.pdf	**Awareness of my body** Teach names of body parts: Look in the mirror and discuss hair colour, eye colour, differences between people. **Awareness of others' bodies** Draw around each other's bodies on a large piece of paper. You can later use these to label body parts. When doing laundry, hold up different items of clothing and use them to talk about different things adults and children wear, and preferences people have for colour/fabric, etc. **Understand the changes that will happen during puberty** Talk about the lifecycle and show photographs and pictures of boys and girls growing up and changing. Use social stories to talk about the changes that will happen to your child. **Awareness of differences in race, gender, sex, age, ability** Talk about differences between people using photographs and pictures. **Ways of expressing gender – masculinity and femininity** Use photographs and magazines to look at images, and use fabrics, smells (perfume, aftershave) and makeup to look at different ways of expressing yourself. Allow children to choose what they wear, and other aspects of their appearance. **Understand parts of the body that are private** Teach the 'underwear rule', (i.e. that the parts of your body covered by your underwear are private, and shouldn't be touched by anyone.) You may need to teach exceptions to this if your child has help with personal care. Use pictures to show parts of the body others can touch, with your permission. Use red and green stickers on the body of a model (doll) to show 'okay' and 'not okay' to touch. Reinforce this message with a social story. **Understand places that are public and private** Use pictures and photographs of different rooms in the house and places outside to show where is public and where is private.

Topic	Aims/targets	Resources	Skills and knowledge
Personal hygiene, periods, public and private	To develop independence skills in managing personal hygiene and menstruation To develop understanding of public and private concepts	Sanitary products Shaving products Deodorant and other hygiene products Symbols to represent periods Social story about managing periods Symbols to represent public and private Family Planning Association (2014) *Periods: What You Need to Know*. London: FPA Rees, M., Carter, C. and Myers, L. (2008) *Periods – A Practical Guide*. Sedbergh: Me-and-Us Ltd Rees, M. Carter, C. and Myers, L. (2008) *I Change My Pad*. Sedbergh: Me-and-Us Ltd The Elfrida Society. *Help! I've Started My Periods*. Available at www.easyhealth.org.uk/listing/periods-(leaflets)	**Skills in using deodorant, washing and looking after skin** Use visual schedules and symbols to explain how these tasks are done and to help with sequencing. Use social stories to explain why these tasks are important. Give children an opportunity to try different products. Practise using models. Start by asking children to try the very last step in a task; then add on one more step at a time until they have learnt the whole sequence. **Understanding periods and what will happen** Use social stories to explain what will happen and why. **Skills in changing and disposing of sanitary products** Show the sanitary products and practise placing pads in underwear and disposing of them correctly. **Skills in shaving** Use social stories to explain what will happen when hair grows and why. Show the objects required for shaving and use visual schedules and symbols to show what needs to happen. **Making decisions about how intimate care happens** Ideally, work with your child and someone who knows them well at school to discuss how they want help (if needed) with personal care. How do they want to communicate about it? What skills do they already have and what do they want to develop? Who do they feel most comfortable with? **Continence skills** Develop a programme to support continence skills (see Chapter 4, Section 4.6).

Topic	Aims/targets	Resources	Skills and knowledge
Private personal touching, masturbation	To develop understanding of different types of touch To identify and communicate about safe touch To develop understanding of masturbation	Different objects to touch and try (e.g. feathers, playdoh, vibrating objects) King, K. (2008) *I Said No: A Kid-to-Kid Guide to Keeping Your Private Parts Private*. Weaverville, CA: Boulden Publishing Reynolds, K. (2014) *Things Tom Likes: A Book About Sexuality and Masturbation for Boys and Young Men with Autism and Related Conditions*. London: Jessica Kingsley Wrobel, M. (2003) *Taking Care of Myself: A Hygiene, Puberty and Personal Curriculum for Young People with Autism*. Arlington, TX: Future Horizons *Jason's Private World* or *Kylie's Private World* – DVDs, available at www.lifesupportproductions.co.uk/jpwdvd.php Leeds Nursing (2009) *Puberty and sexuality for children and young people with a learning disability (a supporting document for national curriculum objectives)*. Leeds: The Children's Learning Disability Nursing Team, available at www.leeds.gov.uk/docs/Puberty-and-Sexuality-Pack-Session1-4.pdf Anatomically correct dolls and condom demonstrators (ejaculating), available at www.bodysense.org.uk/models.shtml	**Preferences for different types of touch (taps, light touch, deep pressure touch, strokes)** Try out different sensory experiences through play and talk about what feels okay and not okay. **Different types of touch for different levels of intimacy (hugs, high fives)** Be explicit about the rules with touch depending on levels of intimacy in relationships. For example, it is okay to have a 'front hug or bear hug' with parents/carers, but most of the time friends prefer 'side hugs'. It is not okay to sit on your teacher's lap. Allow opportunities for touch, such as through swimming, gym, circle games. Safe touch – what is okay and not okay? Link to public and private concepts. Teach children where it is okay to touch people and where it is okay and not okay for people to touch them. Sometimes it can be helpful to teach children 'high fives' if they tend to want to touch people a lot. **Understanding male/female masturbation** It can be helpful to do this teaching in collaboration with school and to develop a plan. First use drawings in the resources recommended and then consider using the DVDs. See Chapter 5.

Topic	Aims/targets	Resources	Skills and knowledge
Positive and safe touch, developing social connections and being with others in friendships/groups	To understand the social rules of touching and different types of touch To develop understanding of different kinds of relationships	Frankel, F. (2010) *Friends Forever: How Parents Can Help Their Kids Make and Keep Good Friends*. San Francisco, CA: John Wiley & Sons Scott, L. and Kerr Edwards, L. (2010) *Talking Together About Growing Up: A Workbook for Parents of Children With Learning Disabilities*. London: Family Planning Association Goodhart, P. (2004). *You Choose!* London: Corgi Children's	**Being with another person in a pair and turn-taking skills** Offer opportunities for play with another person, including physical games (holding hands like 'row row row your boat', parachute games, swimming games). Teach positive touch – high fives, holding hands – and talk about asking for permission for hugs. **Being in a group, initiating play and conversation** Offer opportunities to be with other children and play games with a level of cooperation and physical contact. Teach children how to join in with others (see friendship resources). **Making choices and saying 'yes' and 'no'** Practise making choices about everyday activities. Offer opportunities to say 'yes' and 'no' through play and roleplay, using symbols or words. **Understand differences between friendships, romantic relationships, sexual relationships, marriage** Use social stories, photographs and pictures. Talk about the legal boundaries of sexual relationships (e.g. it is not okay to have a sexual relationship with a carer, someone in your family, or someone under 16).

Topic	Aims/targets	Resources	Skills and knowledge
Sexual relationships, falling in love, consent and contraception	To understand sexual feelings and love/like concepts Understand what sex is Understand what contraception is and how to use it Understand what consent is and making choices about sex Understand the sexual behaviour rules	Magazines and pictures of celebrities Photographs of young person and their family and friends Kerr-Edwards, L. and Scott, L. (2007) *Talking Together About Contraception: A Practical Resource for Parents and Staff Working with Young People with Learning Disabilities.* London: Family Planning Association Kerr-Edwards, L. and Scott, L. (2010) *Talking Together About Sex and Relationships: A Practical Resource for Schools and Parents Working with Young People with Learning Disabilities.* London: Family Planning Association Anatomically correct dolls and condom demonstrators (ejaculating); available at www.bodysense.org.uk/models.shtml	**Understand differences between like, love and crush** Use social stories to explain these concepts. Help children to understand their feelings if you have noticed that they are beginning to develop crushes or sexual feelings towards someone. Look at pictures of people and relationships on TV and in magazines and ask children whether they think the couple are friends or in a romantic relationship, and whether they like, love or have a crush on the other person. **Understand what sex is** Use stories made for young people or the resources recommended to explain what sex is and the specific behaviours involved. **Understand decision making and consent** Help children to know the legal rules around sexual contact. Teach them to say 'no' to unwanted sexual contact and ask for help (see Chapter 8). **Understand what contraception is** Some young people with intellectual disabilities may have the capacity to consent to sex (see Chapter 8). Use the resources recommended to teach about contraception and let them know where they could get it. Some young people will need to practise using and disposing of condoms on a model.

Collaborating with school

Teaching children about relationships and sex is always going to be most effective when it is done in collaboration with those who also have a role in caring for them. We would recommend talking to your child's teacher or headteacher about their approach to RSE.

Our experience is that parents of children with profound disabilities rarely have opportunities to talk with other people in a similar situation, but are often keen to have the chance to discuss how to support their children's sexual rights and needs. The first author (SB) has worked with a special school who provided a discussion group for parents, and used this to develop their curriculum in collaboration with the school community.

Topics and questions for discussion in the parent group included the following:

- What do you think our children need to know about their bodies, sex and relationships?

- How do you think intimate care should be managed?

- The relationships in our children's lives – siblings, friends, parents, personal assistants.

- Personal hygiene and teaching personal care skills.

- Managing menstruation.

- Sexual arousal and masturbation.

- Protecting your child/safeguarding from abuse.

- Touch and greetings.

- Peer relationships and friendships.

- Body and behaviour changes.

- Becoming an adult.

Supporting young people with intellectual disabilities to learn the skills they need to enjoy romantic relationships and to experience their sexuality safely is an important issue. They will have the same core feelings as young people without disabilities, yet they often do not get the support and guidance they need to help them understand what is happening in their bodies and to learn how to behave towards other people. We hope that this book, based on questions asked by parents, has provided some useful information about the challenges faced by young people with intellectual disabilities and their families and some practical guidance on how to overcome them.

Sexuality is a complex topic and most parents will feel a natural uncertainty and hesitation when taking up the challenge of providing sex and relationships education for their children. The task is even harder, but potentially all the more important, for parents of children with intellectual disabilities. But it is important to remember that you do not need to do it alone and if after reading this book you are still struggling with what to do and how to do it, then contact your local community health and social services for further advice and support.

REFERENCES

Albanese, A. and Hopper, N. W. (2007) 'Suppression of menstruation in adolescents with severe learning disabilities.' *Archives of Disease in Childhood 92*, 7, 629–632.

Azrin, N. H. and Foxx, R. M. (1989) *Toilet Training in Less Than a Day: A Tested Method for Teaching Your Child Quickly and Happily!* London: Pocket Books.

BBC3 (2009) *Otto: Love, Lust and Las Vegas.* BBC3, 21 July 2009.

Brown, H. and Craft, A. (1989) 'Thinking the unthinkable: Papers on sexual abuse and people with learning disabilities.' London: Family Planning Association.

Carnaby, S. (2006) 'Adults with Profound and Multiple Learning Disabilties – Supporting Planned Dependence.' In S. Carnaby and P. Cambridge (eds) *Intimate and Personal Care with People with Learning Disabilities.* London: Jessica Kingsley Publishers.

Craft, A. (1987). Mental handicap and sexuality: issues for individuals with a mental handicap, their parents and professionals. In Craft, A. (ed.) Mental Handicap and Sexuality: Issues and Perspectives. Tunbridge Wells: Costello.

Department of Health (2005) *Mental Capacity Act.* London: HMSO.

Department of Health (2009) *Valuing People Now: A New Three-Year Strategy for People with Learning Disabilities.* London: The Stationery Office.

Department of Justice (2003) *Sexual Offences Act.* HMSO, London.

Enthoven, G. (2011) *Come as you are.* Fobic Films: Belgium.

Forced Marriage Unit (2009) *Multiagency Practice Guidelines: Handling Cases of Forced Marriage.* London: HM Government.

Frankel, F. (2010) *Friends Forever: How Parents Can Help Their Kids Make and Keep Friends.* San Francisco, CA: Jossey-Bass.

Gray, C. (2015) *The New Social Story Book* (revised and expanded 15th anniversary edition). Arlington, TX: Future Horizons.

HMSO (2003) *Sexual Offences Act.* London: HMSO.

Jones, C. (2012) 'Paying for sex: The many obstacles in the way of men with learning disabilities using prostitutes.' *British Journal of Learning*

King, K. (2008) *I Said No: A Kid-to-Kid Guide to Keeping Your Private Parts Private.* Weaverville, CA: Boulden Publishing.

Leeds Nursing (2009) *Puberty and sexuality for children and young people with a learning disability (a supporting document for national curriculum objectives).* Leeds: The Children's Learning Disability Nursing Team.

Mental Capacity Act (2005). Available at www.legislation.gov.uk/ukpga/2005/9/contents, accessed 2 April 2016.

McCarthy, M. (1999*) Sexuality and Women with Learning Disabilities.* London: Jessica Kingsley.

McCarthy, M. (2010) 'The Sexual Lives of Women with Learning Disabilities.' In G. Grant, P. Ramcharan, M. Flynn and M. Richardson (eds) *Learning Disability: A Lifecycle Approach* (2nd edition). Milton Keynes: Open University Press.

Miller, N. B. (1994) *Nobody's Perfect: Living and Growing with Children Who Have Special Needs.* Baltimore, MD: Paul H. Brookes Publishing Co.

Mosley, J. and Grogan, R. (2008) *The Big Book of Calmers.* Trowbridge: Positive Press.

NSPCC (2015) *Simple conversations to help keep your child safe from abuse.* NSPCC: England, Wales and Scotland. Available at www.nspcc.org.uk/underwear, accessed 9 April 2016.

Parker, V. (2007) *The Little Book of Growing Up.* London: Hodder.

Reynolds, K. (2015) *What's Happening to Ellie? A Book about Puberty for Girls and Young Women with Autism and Related Conditions.* London: Jessica Kingsley.

Rice, C., Renooy, L., Zitzelsberger, H., Aubin, A. and Odette, F. (2003) *Talking About Body Image, Identity, Disability and Difference: A Facilitator's Manual.* Ontario: Building Bridges.

Stopes, M. (1918) *Married* Love. London: Fifield & Co.

Toates, F, (2014) *How Sexual Desire Works: The Enigmatic Urge.* Cambridge University Press.

UK Youth Parliament (2007) *Sex and Relationships Education: Are You Getting It?* London: UK Youth Parliament. Available at www.ukyouthparliament.org.uk, accessed 2 April 2016.

Wrobel, M. (2003) *Taking Care of Myself: A Hygiene, Puberty and Personal Curriculum for Young People with Autism.* Arlington, TX: Future Horizons.

CPSIA information can be obtained
at www.ICGtesting.com
Printed in the USA
FFOW02n0503070616
24740FF